A Cook's Tour of Mexico

Authentic Recipes from the Country's Best Open-Air Markets, City Fondas, and Home Kitchens

MEATLESS MEXICAN HOME COOKING

MEATLESS MEXICAN HOME COOKING

Traditional Recipes
That Celebrate the Regional Flavors
of Mexico

Nancy Zaslavsky

DRAWINGS BY MORRIS ZASLAVSKY

ST. MARTIN'S PRESS

NEW YORK

MEATLESS MEXICAN HOME COOKING

Design by Ultragraphics, Venice, California

Library of Congress Cataloging-in-Publication Data
Zaslavsky, Nancy.
Meatless Mexican home cooking / Nancy Zaslavsky.
p.   cm.
Includes index.
ISBN 0-312-15170-5
1. Vegetarian cookery. 2. Cookery, Mexican. I. Title.
TX837.Z38   1997
641.5'636'0972—dc20   96-27461
CIP

First Edition: April 1997
10 9 8 7 6 5 4 3 2 1

Acknowledgments

This book is dedicated to the memory of my mother, Frances Niedhammer,
who was the best cook on the block.

FRIENDS IN MEXICO MADE THIS BOOK POSSIBLE. I THANK EACH and every one of them. Without their boundless spirit and generous support this collection of traditional meatless recipes would not have come to be. Food experts throughout Mexico unselfishly shared recipes and secrets from old files and bound volumes. Most often, though, great Mexican home cooks recited by memory exactly how their grandmothers prepared these family favorites. Many of these recipes were written down for the very first time, and the fact that they were translated and printed in English—in a gringo cookbook of all places—delighted more than one *amigo*. The name above a recipe is very important to me—it's the name of a Mexican friend who donated that particular family treasure. I especially would like to thank people who worked above and beyond the call of duty: two champions of good taste in Pátzcuaro, Michoacán, Doña Esperanza de Sepulveda and Marilyn Mayo; San Miguel de Allende's Reyna Polanco Abrahams and Mercedes Arteaga Tovar; and Soledad Díaz Altamirano of Oaxaca's El Topil restaurant. Thank you also Pilar Cabrera, Jana Napoli, and Marcela López Brun.

Thank you to Rosario Chávez and Soledad López de Wittrock, who have been inspirations to me in my quest for superb quality and superb taste. Particular thanks to special friends Kim and Michael McCarty, Steve Smith, Mary and John Bragg, Monica

Grinnell, Marilyn Gilbaugh, Nancy Lamb, Angela Rinaldi, and Marlies and Rick Najaka.

Friends who gave their all by tasting first-run recipe tests and are still around to prove it: Lulee Fisher and Steve McGlothen, Gary Praglin and Synthia Schechner, Jeanne and John Binder, Danna and Ed Ruscha, Donna Vaccarino, Robin and Maurice Vaccarino, Gwen and Chas Garabedian, Fritzy Roeder, Tressa Miller and Bill Schwartz, Judy and Marvin Zeidler, Mike Perlis, Ruth and Ron Amen, Nan Sheri Lieberman, Tom Yasuda and Pat Henk, Janie Hewson and Victor Budnick, C.P. Pulitzer and James Polster, Patricia and Franklin Melton, Marny Randall, Susan Lieberman, Jeannine Oppewall, Marsha and Richard Tatro, Pat and David Veriepe, Kathryn Peters and Ben Cardinale, Emily Jennings, Barbara Essick and Chic Mendez, and Kimberly and David Tyson.

Morris Zaslavsky, my husband and biggest supporter (plus longest-running food taster), did the outstanding drawings for this book, and I thank him with all my heart. Other family members constantly encourage my efforts and I send a hug to Herbert and Gwen Niedhammer, Susan and Larry Phelps, Warren and Karen Niedhammer, Marilyn and Bert Friedlieb, and Renate and Skip Fitch.

My editors at St. Martin's Press: Thank you again, Barbara Anderson, for your insight and encouragment, and thank you to Marian Lizzi for keeping everything in focus. Thank you to my agent, Angela Miller.

Contents

Introduction

IN THE COMING MILLENNIUM, MEXICAN FOOD WILL BE AS ABUNDANT and as popular as Italian food is now. Back in the 1950s just about every town in the U.S.A. had an Italian joint serving spaghetti swimming in tomato sauce. Adored by children and adults alike, basic red-sauce spaghetti and meatballs, lasagne, ravioli, and pizza became buzz words for good times and good eats. Always delectable, cheap, filling, and fun, these classics have given way to equally scrumptious and soul-satisfying Mexican dishes. Basic red sauce also enhances corn-based dishes, but, most important, it contains Mexico's high-spirited ingredient—chile. Marinara, move over. Salsa's coming on strong.

Mexican food no longer translates to spicy, greasy border-town grub. It's time to get aquainted with Mexico's sophisticated, centuries-old cuisine, which is gaining an international reputation. *Meatless Mexican Home Cooking* is a collection of generously spiced, exuberantly flavored, vegetarian dishes from great Mexican cooks. Meatless here means no red meat, poultry, or fish, but does include dairy products and eggs. Recipes are old Mexican family treasures or personal favorites of mine. The recipes are easy to make, with most ingredients easy to find, and they provide good, honest plates of food. Waves of recent Mexican immigrants are forcing supermarkets and restaurants across the U.S.A. to offer products and dishes unheard of five years ago. Tortillas are now baked fresh every day in neighborhood tortillerías (and *masa harina,* treated corn flour, is stocked at your supermarket); fresh and dried chiles are standard produce items; exotic tropical fruits are almost as common as apples and bananas; and Mexican-style cheeses are stocked in dairy cases across the country. *Meatless Mexican Home Cooking* is packed with authentic, traditional preparations rather than gringo variations on Mexican standards. You won't find typical health-food Mexican vegetarian recipes that rely on tofu and soy burgers to substitute for meat. You *will* find flavorful, uncomplicated, unpretentious meatless regional foods popular throughout Mexico. They're all healthful, fresh, and delicious.

Don't be quick to assume Mexican food is synonymous with grilled steak, lard-filled beans, fatty meat tacos, and insanely spicy pork stews. You have to experience central and southern Mexico's delicious sauces made from nuts, seeds, chiles, fruit, and sometimes chocolate, spooned over rice pilafs; corn dough tartlets filled with exotically flavored pink beans; or toasted chiles stuffed with grilled vegetables and luscious melted cheeses—one taste and you'll be hooked forever. A tamale made without lard or animal products will turn you into a fan, especially with fillings such as: green olives, capers, raisins, and chipotle chiles; sweet papaya or mango with ground nuts in the corn dough; and plantains, orange juice, and habanero chile wrapped in banana leaves.

Traditional recipes can easily be translated into low-fat or even nonfat dishes. Cut the suggested oil and cook in nonstick pots and skillets. Low-fat dairy products are everywhere, so use them! The flavor won't be exactly as in Mexico but it wouldn't be even if you use a full-fat product. We're not living in Mexico, and our local cheeses, creams, vegetables, herbs, and fruits are different from Mexican counterparts simply because they're grown or produced in a different locale. Just as a sauce made in San Diego won't taste exactly the same as one cooked from an identical fresh ingredient in Boston because of the soil, fertilizers, irrigation methods, natural humidity levels, and general plant care, the equivalent idea is true in Mexico.

Wherever you live and whatever variations you decide to make with these recipes, remember that meatless doesn't mean bland and boring anymore.

Chiles

CHILE GIVES MEXICAN FOOD ITS DYNAMIC PERSONALITY. MORE than corn, tortillas, tomatoes, or even beans, it's chile that makes a Mexican meal sing out with a mariachi marathon of mouth explosions. There are hundreds of varieties of chiles grown in Mexico today, all descendants of those grown by Mayans and Aztecs thousands of years ago. Even though chiles may be the new kids on the block when talking about ingredients for most western cuisines, they've been around almost since the beginning of time and are native to South America. Genus *Capsicum* includes all peppers, from the mild bell pepper we use for stuffing and slicing raw into salads, to one of the world's hottest examples, the Yucatán peninsula's habanero chile.

▶ ▶ ▶ ▶ ▶ ▶ ▶ ▶ ▶ ▶ ▶ ▶ ▶ ▶

Chiles

Chiles are similar to herbs in cooking—they make simple dishes stand up and be noticed, thanks to their particular flavor variations. Distinctive herbs such as tarragon, dill, and rosemary are great examples of how a spoonful alters a dish's taste completely. What makes one chile different from another is its flavor, not hotness, as many people think. Berry, coffee, apricot, tobacco, grass, and citrus are a few terms used to summarize the nuances of chiles—descriptions not unlike those reserved for fine wines. Try this easy test: First, buy a bag of unflavored corn tortilla chips and invite a few friends over. Next, transform a simple salsa of chopped tomatoes, sweet onions, and lime juice by adding fresh jalapeño chiles to a small portion. That combination is completely modified by substituting soaked, dried anchos for the jalapeños in another portion. The taste will again vary by switching chipotles for the anchos, and again by swapping habaneros for chipotles. When you've mastered well-known chiles, graduate to the subtle dried varieties found in Mail-Order Sources (page 204), and by all means experiment with toasted (page 28) verses untoasted chiles. Spiciness is not the goal; tone down heat by adding the tiniest smidgen of each chile. You can always add more. This is one cooking experiment that's easy and fun, and that makes you feel great, too.

Chiles are an original feel-good food, and eating them is addictive. Capsaicin (the natural spice) in fresh or dried chiles causes nerves in the mouth to send S.O.S. signals to the brain. In return, the brain sends out endorphins, which produce a feeling of well being, even euphoria if enough is released. Long-distance runners claim the feeling to be worth any exercise agony. So, the more spicy chile you eat, the more endorphins are set free. Hallelujah! Praise the Lord and pass the chiles.

Capsaicin, along with other less well-known chemicals, causes the heat that's associated with chiles. Too often a dish is overly spicy because the cook used far too much chile and masked intricate flavors. Or, more typically, the diner splashed bottled hot sauce over his or her food and obliterated any taste at all. Generally, the smaller the chile, the hotter it is. The Scoville test, which measures the strength of a chile by dilutability, is the chilehead's bible. A ranking of 10,000 means you can put a piece of chile in 10,000 times as much slightly sweetened water and still taste hotness.

Chiles are used in both fresh and dried forms. To complicate matters, a fresh chile often has a different name from its dried version. If certain chiles are unavailable in your area, even by mail order, substituting is easy. Substitute a fresh green chile for another fresh green chile—for example, a serrano is slightly smaller and spicier than a jalapeño, yet the two are exchanged regularly throughout Mexico; tiny hot dried chiles for other tiny hot dried chiles; exchange smoky dried morita chiles for smoky dried chipotle chiles; or exchange fresh yellow for yellow, and red for red. Taste your chiles—sometimes one chile is much spicier than another, so keep this in mind when making salsas. The only canned chiles I recommend are *chipotles en adobo* and pickled jalapeños.

Many people wear rubber gloves while cleaning chiles because chiles are very strong for those with sensitive skin. Thin medical gloves can be purchased in any drugstore and are superior to standard kitchen gloves. If you don't wear gloves, wash your hands often with soap when preparing large amounts of chiles. Never touch your face, especially your eyes—they will burn and tear for hours.

Fresh chiles

When choosing fresh chiles:
• Look for green stems and hard, firm surfaces.
• All chiles should feel heavy for their size.
• Brown stems and soft or wrinkled skins mean the chiles are old and could be moldy or dried-out inside, and therefore flavorless.
• Chiles change color as they ripen. Bell peppers, jalapeños, and serranos are picked either green or red. Habaneros are picked green, yellow, or orange.
• Chiles left on the vine until they are red-ripe have a less biting, raw flavor and many people claim they are easier to digest.
• Pick the color you want your sauce to be: Red for red tomato sauces and green for green sauces made with tomatillos.
• Be aware that in a bag of any fresh chiles there will always be a few that are hotter than the rest—or maybe a dud with no heat at all.

Gordo Huachinango. Large ripe, red jalapeño with thin white lines running vertically. Dried to make the largest and most pricey chipotle, the meco. Sweet, spicy flavor.

Güero. A generic name for yellow chiles. Hungarian wax pepper, a.k.a. banana chile. With waxy texture, it looks like a yellow jalapeño. Called largo or carricillo chile when pickled. On the Yucatán peninsula a yellow chile is the sweet, thin-fleshed xcatick or chawa chile, measuring about 5 inches long. Substitute jalapeño chile for flavor, or a combination of yellow habanero and yellow bell pepper for color.

Habanero. Mexico's hottest. Delicate-looking green, yellow, and orange "lanterns" are prized by Yucatecos for their hotter-than-hell fire. Green are crispest, orange softest, with a ripe chile flavor. Use a tiny ½-inch piece the first time you cook with habanero chile—you can always add more. The special fruity flavor complements fresh salsas made with tropical fruits.

Jalapeño. The most widely used fresh, green (ripens to red) chile in Mexico and the United States. About 3 inches long by ¾ inch wide. Solid vegetable flavor. Ripened and smoked, it becomes the chipotle chile. Also known as cuaresmeño chile in Mexico City. Substitute the smaller, but spicier, serrano chile.

Macho. Tiny, long chiles with a macho bang. Green or red. Substitute fresh de árbol chile.

Perón. A.k.a. manzano and rocoto chile. Looks like a cross between a small, yellow bell pepper and golden habanero. Medium to hot and is at its peak of popularity in the state of Michoacán. It has black seeds and the flower is purple. Fruity, tropical flavor with a bit of citrus. Thin flesh.

Poblano. Dark green with meaty, thick flesh. The prerequisite for chiles rellenos. Always cooked, never used raw. Dried, it's an ancho chile. (Only in California are the fresh poblano chile and dried ancho chile both called pasilla chile.) Mild to slightly spicy. Strong vegetable flavor of green beans. Substitute the longer, thinner, lighter green Anaheim chile.

Serrano. Next to the jalapeño, Mexico's most popular fresh green chile—the two are often interchangeable. A thickly fleshed serrano is slightly hotter than the larger jalapeño. Its size is about 2 inches long by ½ inch wide. Ripened and dried, a serrano becomes a very hot serrano seco, a.k.a. morita chile in some regions. Morita chiles are also smoked.

Dried chiles

Mexico's best-known dried chiles are listed here. There are dozens more, not counting hundreds from the United States and other countries.

When choosing dried chiles:

• Pick up and bend a dried ancho, mulato, chipotle, or exotic Oaxacan pasilla chile. Each has the texture of fruit leather—their skins are wrinkled and pliable.

• Other dried chiles such as guajillo, cascabel, and de árbol have smooth, brittle, thin skins.

• Rock-hard chiles are fine to use, they need only to be soaked longer to reconstitute. Years-old chipotle chiles may need to be soaked for 24 hours.

• You may microwave chiles in a damp paper towel for about 30 seconds to soften.

Ancho. The most popular dried chile in Mexico and the United States. It's a dried poblano chile. The deep cordovan-colored, wrinkled body has wide shoulders that taper to a point. Smoky-sweet flavor of dried fruit and redolent of anise, the ancho accents numerous dishes. Mild heat. Substitute mulato chile.

Cascabel. Richly flavored, 1-inch round brown chile from central Mexico, especially Michoacán. It's also called bola chile, because of its ball shape. When shaken, the loose seeds make it sound like a rattle. *(Cascabel* means rattle in Spanish.) Flavor is nutty, slightly smoky, and acidic. Medium to hot.

Chipotle. Ripened and smoked jalapeño chile, it's also called an ahumado chile. Fiery hot with lasting smoky flavor. Chipotle meco, the largest, is a dried gordo huachinango chile. It's smoked in a special humid environment and has a medium brown, suedelike surface. Chipotle mora is cordovan-colored with a fruit-leather texture and slightly more sweet than chipotle meco. This midsized jalapeño is lightly smoked and often used for canned *chiles chipotles en adobo*. Morita is the last picking from the plants and always smallest, with the same characteristics as mora.

Chipotle chiles en adobo. Dried midsized chipotle chiles that have been reconstituted in a chile sauce (see page 44). Clemente Jacques and San Marcos are good canned brands because they have less tomato sauce filler than others, and therefore more chile flavor.

de Árbol. Red, small (about 3 inches long), and pointed—with a searing heat. Used in bottled hot sauces. It's the cayenne powder chile; dried, it's de árbol seco. Thin-fleshed with brittle skin. Substitute pequín chile or any tiny, red hot chile.

FRESH PERON CHILE (A.K.A. MANZANO CHILE)

Guajillo. Large, 5 inches long by over 1 inch wide. Deep cordovan to medium brown with a thin skin. Mild to medium heat and very popular throughout Mexico. Fruity, citrusy flavors. Substitute dried California or New Mexican chiles.

Holy Trinity. You'll hear this term often when talking about black *mole*. Three dried chiles necessary for the classic sauce are: true pasilla chile (a.k.a. negro chile); mulato chile; and ancho chile (if you can't get the hard-to-find chilhuacle negro chile of Oaxaca).

Mulato. A type of dried poblano chile, very similar to the ancho chile in looks and taste but with slightly more tart, dusky smoke and anise flavor, with overtones of bitter chocolate. It's used to make *mole* poblano (from Puebla) and *mole* negro (from Oaxaca). Dark black with a fruit leather texture.

Pasilla. Long, 7 inches by 1 inch wide. The dried chilaca chile is also called negro chile. Raisin-black with a thin, fruit leather–like pliable, wrinkled skin. Slightly spicier than ancho and mulato chiles but with similar dried fruit and sun-dried tomato overtones. This chile is not the dried poblano chile mistakingly called pasilla chile in California.

Pasilla de Oaxaca. Sold by one hundred pieces (not by weight like other chiles) in various sizes, and only in Oaxaca markets by specialty vendors who sell these chiles and no others. They are available by mail order (see page 204). The expensive chiles are deep cordovan red, fruit leather textured, and smoky-flavored (from smoking over beds of ferns). Not quite so hot or smoky as a chipotle chile. A.k.a. mije chile in Oaxaca.

Piquín. Very hot, tiny, orange-red, oval chiles. Thin flesh that crumbles easily. Often ground into powder and sprinkled on grilled corn and fruit sold by street vendors. Substitute any small, hot chile peppers.

Chile powder. Chile-powder blends and single-variety powders are available. Be sure the product is pure chile powder and not a blend of chile, salt, sugar, pepper, and paprika.

Masa and Tortillas

TORTILLAS ARE THE BREAD OF MEXICO. THERE IS NOTHING quite as wonderful as air scented with hot corn tortillas fresh off a *comal*. Handmade tortillas are far superior to store-bought, or even those made in a tortillería. One age-old method, and most exquisite, is the difficult-to-master technique of hand-pat-patting corn *masa* or wheat dough until thin pancakes are formed. A faster system squashes dough in a tortilla press to form the thin pancakes. What could be better eating than a freshly made tortilla, corn or flour, folded around a dazzling chile-enhanced mixture?

Corn Tortillas
Tortillas de Maiz

Great Mexican food begins with absolutely fresh corn tortillas. Years ago (and in pueblos today) traditional *masa*-making was a labor-intensive ritual that cooks in every Mexican household went through daily. *Masa* (corn dough) is made from kernels of dried corn. Large, starchy, dried field corn kernels (similar to hominy) are heated and soaked overnight in water with slaked, chemically pure lime (calcium hydroxide, called *cal* in Spanish) that needs to be diluted in water. Lime makes field corn easier to digest by dissolving the outer hull. An added nutritional bonus is that lime adds calcium to corn. (Lime is bitter-tasting and should be kept away from your eyes.) Next, you rub the soaked kernels between your hands under running water until the chaff slips off. Then you either hand-grind the kernels on a lava grinding stone with a lava tool, or take the treated kernels to a neighborhood mill and have them stone-ground to your specific texture. Fresh *masa* should be used immediately because it sours quickly; it may be refrigerated and also be frozen, but it will never be as heavenly as fresh. Refrigerated *masa* makes chewy tortillas.

Today we have the option to buy fresh *masa* at tortillerías in Latino communities, or to make *masa* from instant, dry *masa harina* (lime-treated corn flour)—it is to be mixed with water and reconstituted back into corn dough. A spokesperson at The Quaker Oats Company told me that if you ask the manager of any large chain supermarket to special-order a bag of *masa harina*, Quaker will send it at no additional charge. Maseca-brand *masa harina* is now available in two grinds: fine for tortillas and coarse for tamales. Like so much in Mexican cooking, texture is everything. It may be fine for us to make tortillas with *masa harina*, but traditionalists are livid over this newfangled instant stuff. *Masa* made from *masa harina* lacks the elasticity of fresh *masa;* it often crumbles, making thin tortillas a chore.

Masa harina is very different from the cornmeal we're used to in the United States. The U.S.-Mexico border is also the cornmeal–*masa harina* border: Southern cooks would never think of preparing any of their umpteen cornmeal recipes with *masa harina,* just as Mexican cooks wouldn't know what to do with our cornmeal. Cornmeal is ground dried corn that hasn't been soaked in lime. The products and textures are completely different, so never use cornmeal to prepare *masa.*

Yield: 12 tortillas

For masa:

2 cups *masa harina* (fine-grind instant corn *masa* mix)

1⅛ cups water

½ teaspoon kosher salt

Tortilla press

2 plastic sandwich bags larger than the tortilla press

1. Purchase 1 pound *masa* at a tortillería and add warm water until the dough becomes pliable, or make *masa* using *masa harina:* With your hands, mix the *masa harina,* 1 cup water, and salt thoroughly for 2 to 3 minutes, until the dough forms a soft ball. If the dough feels dry, add 1 tablespoon water at a time and mix again.

2. Cover the bowl with a towel and let the corn dough rest for 5 minutes while you heat a *comal* (metal or earthenware cooking disk), griddle, or heavy skillet to very hot.

3. Either use a rolling pin to roll tortillas into 5- to 6-inch circles or use a tortilla press: Put a bag on the bottom part of your tortilla press. The extra thickness of the bag works better than a flimsy sheet of plastic wrap.

4. Pull off a walnut-sized piece of *masa,* roll it into a ball, then flatten it into a 2-inch thick disk. Center it on the bag that's placed on the press. Cover the *masa* with another bag. Lower the top of the press and push down on the handle— less hard for thicker, smaller tortillas (good for *Sopes,* page 60), or harder for thin tortillas. Open the press, turn the tortilla 180 degrees, and push harder this second time.

5. Open the press. The tortilla will have a bag stuck on the top and one on the bottom. Peel away the top plastic, then flip the tortilla over into your other hand and carefully peel that plastic away. If there are cracks along the edges, the dough is too dry and a little more water must be kneaded in.

6. Slowly lay the tortilla on the very hot ungreased *comal,* griddle, or skillet. The tortilla should make a small sizzle. When it starts to unstick after 15 seconds, turn the tortilla over and continue to cook for another 30 to 40 seconds as it looks speckled brown underneath. Turn again and cook for another 20 to 30 seconds. It will puff like pita bread. Remove the hot tortilla to a napkin-lined basket to keep warm and pliable, then continue with the rest of the dough.

White Flour Tortillas
Tortillas de Harina

Flour tortillas, the pride of northern Mexico, range in size from standard 8 to 10 inches up to 24-inch burrito-sized monsters—just right for an entire wrapped meal for a small family. Average-sized flour tortillas are slightly larger than corn tortillas; freshly made, their delicate taste and texture provide the consummate edible envelope. Tortillas hot off the stove, no matter how badly misshapen, taste fabulous. When serving, don't choose the top tortilla, but dig down and take one from the center of the napkin-wrapped pile where they are the warmest and most moist, as do all Mexicans.

Yield: 12 tortillas

2 cups unbleached flour

1 teaspoon kosher salt

½ cup vegetable shortening

⅓ to ½ cup water

1. Put the flour and salt in a large bowl. With two knives, cut the shortening into the flour until the mixture resembles oatmeal. Add half the water, working it into the flour with your hand. Continue adding water until the dough becomes firm, shiny, and elastic. It should not be sticky. If the dough is sticky, add additional flour and knead it for a few minutes more.

2. Cover the dough with plastic wrap and put it in the refrigerator for about 20 minutes for the gluten to relax. Meanwhile, heat a *comal,* griddle, or nonstick skillet to very hot.

3. Form the dough into 12 balls. Place them on a tray and cover with plastic wrap. Refrigerate 10 minutes. Pat a ball into a 4-inch circle. On a floured surface, roll it out to a thin 8-inch circle with a floured rolling pin, rotating and flipping it over as you roll.

4. Carefully place the tortilla on the hot *comal.* Cook for 30 to 40 seconds, flip when the bottom is splotchy brown, and cook for 30 seconds more. Place the tortilla in a napkin-lined basket to keep warm. Repeat with the remaining tortillas.

Notes: Whole wheat flour can be used for tortillas. Mix ¼ cup gluten flour with 1¾ cups whole wheat pastry flour so the dough is smooth and elastic.

Tortillas (corn or flour) keep for up to one week if refrigerated and tightly wrapped, but they never taste so heavenly as when they are freshly made. My favorite way to reheat a tortilla is to put it directly on a gas burner for about 10 seconds, flip it over, and cook for another 10 seconds. You can also reheat it on a *comal,* griddle, or in a heavy skillet. For a slightly stale tortilla, dip it in a bowl of water, then place it on a *comal* for about 15 seconds, flip it over, and cook for another 15 seconds. For 1 dozen tortillas, wrap the stack in a tea towel and steam over simmering water about 12 minutes. You can also wrap a dozen or so in foil and bake at 350°F for 12 minutes. With the steaming and oven methods, be sure the tortillas in the middle are warm.

TORTILLA BASKET

Sauces

SHOVE OVER, HEINZ 57, AND MOVE YOUR KETCHUP TO A LOWER shelf—salsa is now the numero uno condiment in the U.S.A. Smart marketing moves for the right product at the right time certainly helped, because salsa's nonfat, chile-packed flavors for the diet conscious make it irresistible and addictive. Throughout Mexico, uncooked table salsa is known simply as *salsa, salsa fresca,* or *salsa cruda.* When folks from the U.S. hear the word *salsa* they picture lumpy, mushy hot stuff from a jar. When Mexicans hear the word *salsa* they picture a bowl of hand-chopped and ripe-red tomatoes, crunchy onions, fresh chiles, and lime juice that's on everyone's dining table.

Beginning with this basic formula, salsa leaps to new flavor heights thanks to ingredients such as tomatillos, citrus juices, avocados, cilantro, garlic, radishes, cabbage, peanuts, potatoes, nuts, seeds, squash, and all kinds of tropical fruits. But, it's chile that makes salsa sing. Fresh and dried chiles, mild to searingly spicy, turn a bowl of vegetables into explosive tastes you never thought your tongue knew about. Spoon table salsa on almost any gringo food and—*¡ole!*—it's reborn as Mexican.

Sauces

Toasting will lead you to still other dimensions of salsa making. (The Spanish word *salsa* translates to *sauce* and includes both raw and cooked sauces.) A key to the great cooked salsas of southern Mexico, especially *moles* from the indigenous people of Oaxaca and Chiapas, is *toasting* raw ingredients. A *comal* (or heavy skillet, cast iron is best) is kept in a permanent position atop a stove burner because it's used every day. The *comal* is heated to very hot and raw vegetables are placed on its ungreased surface. The vegetables toast, char, and develop black spots, which produce the same flavors of centuries ago when vegetables were placed directly on hot coals. Some vegetable skins are peeled after toasting, others are left on for sauces with smoky, earthy flavors.

When toasting fresh chiles:
- Fresh poblano chiles are never eaten raw. They're toasted, sweated, and peeled before being used in recipes. Large poblanos are toasted directly on gas or electric burners and turned with metal tongs.
- Toast all fresh chiles until blackened—really blackened—all over, with few green areas, or the chile won't peel.
- If you're toasting many chiles for a large recipe, put them directly on a hot grill, or lay them on a baking sheet and broil until the chiles are blackened, turning with tongs.
- Once chiles are blackened, immediately put them in a plastic bag, or in a bowl covered with a kitchen towel, to "sweat" so their skins loosen in the steam they emit.
- Sometimes you'll run into a tough chile that won't shed its skin. Hold it under running warm water and the skin will come off. You'll lose a little flavor but it's not worth the aggravation of peeling around bumps with a paring knife if you have many to peel.
- Toasting is a hallmark of Mexican home cooking at its best. All fresh chiles are toasted to enrich salsa flavors, but many people don't toast chiles or other vegetables—it's all personal and traditional. Many restaurants never toast ingredients simply because the step takes time, and time is money...or the cooks are lazy.

When toasting dried chiles:
- To stem, seed, devein, and toast a dried chile, first cut off the stem end just below the

stem, including the hard clump of seeds.

• Then vertically cut open the chile from stem to point.

• Shake or scrape out the seeds.

• Lay the chile flat and scrape off the lighter-colored veins running vertically on the inside surface—often these veins are spicier than the seeds. If you like spicy food, don't remove the veins—most Mexicans don't.

• Now toast the chile to develop flavor and to remove any bitterness. Toast on both sides on a *comal* or in a heavy skillet, pressing down with a metal spatula. Do not burn. Toast only until the chile color darkens slightly.

• Put the toasted chile in a bowl of hot water to soften.

• Many recipes don't call for toasting dried chiles, even though I feel this step brings out the best qualities in any chile. After, soak the chiles for about 30 minutes in hot water until they are soft. Stem, seed, then blend into one of the sauces starting on page 31.

• Store all dried chiles in a cool, dry place—I store all mine in a freezer, in plastic freezer bags. Bugs love dried chiles and freezing is the best way to keep them totally safe from greedy critters.

When toasting other vegetables:

• You'll see directions to toast, sweat, then peel in most Mexican tomato sauce recipes. Once tomato skins are totally blackened (they look burnt all over), put them in a plastic bag to "sweat" for a few minutes. The black skins loosen and peel or rub off easily.

• Tomatillos are husked then toasted—they are never peeled.

• Onions are halved or quartered and toasted before peeling and grinding.

• Garlic cloves are toasted in their skins, then the skins slip off easily.

• Nuts are toasted for a minute or so until golden.

• Seeds take about 10 seconds until their oils and aromas are released. Toasting seeds and spices always reminds me of Indian cooking and the way heavenly *garam masala* begins with toasting to bring out flavors by extracting their oils with heat.

Texture is a key element of Mexican cooking, especially with sauces. Sauces taste different depending on whether the same ingredients are chopped coarse or fine, or coarsely or finely ground, puréed, or strained. For example, traditionalists mourn the passing of *molca-*

jete-ground sauces, but great cooks still use the labor-intensive, lava-rock grinding bowls and pestles for special-occasion dishes. For small amounts of spices the system has no equal.

When texture is everything:

• Indian women in small pueblos grind their lime-soaked corn for *masa* on a lava grinding slab, a *metate,* daily. They rub a *mano,* or rolling-pin–shaped lava grinding stone, over the kernels until a dough is formed.

• Hand grinding on stone squashes ingredients—a blender or processor cuts ingredients. Contemporary cooks use blenders (processors are seldom seen in Mexico) but everyone appreciates the superb texture stone grinding produces.

• Beans of the cacao tree *(Theobroma cacao)* are ground with a small fire underneath a *metate* so that the heat extracts their oils for better chocolate.

• Because texture is everything, few Mexican sauces are completely smooth. Hardly a salsa passes through a sieve or food mill, and the few that are can generally be spotted in city restaurants.

Frying is the final step in making a cooked salsa. Once you have toasted, sweated, and skinned your vegetables, plus blended eveything into a liquid, it's time to fry the sauce.

When frying the puréed vegetables:

• Oil is heated in a deep pot to very hot, almost smoking, and the ground liquid is poured in (it splatters!).

• A deep pot is necessary, even for a small amount of sauce, because the salsa bubbles and splatters all over your stove if you use anything shallower. (Terracotta-colored dried chile splatter is horrible to clean, trust me.)

• Stir the liquid in the hot oil for a minute, turn down the heat, and simmer, uncovered, until the sauce changes color and becomes darker.

• Simmering time varies depending upon the ingredients, but 20 to 30 minutes is typical, with up to 2 hours for some complicated *moles.*

Basic Uncooked Tomato Table Salsa
Salsa Fresca de Jitomate

Small bowls of spicy salsas are the hallmarks of Mexican food, and regional salsas are cherished in every city and pueblo across the country. The vivid, refreshing taste of a salsa is a perfect match to long-simmered sauces or melted cheese dishes. They act as crunchy textural contrasts with additional flavor layers of spice. Mexico's fresh salsa can easily be compared to Indian chutney—the variations are limitless but the inclusion is mandatory to every meal. One of the most well-known table salsas, Basic Uncooked Tomato Table Salsa, is called *pico de gallo* around the U.S.-Mexican border. The name is derived from how people pick at the chunky mixture and how similar it looks to how chickens pick at feed. *Yield: about 2 cups*

3 red-ripe tomatoes, cored and chopped

1 large white onion, chopped

3 garlic cloves, chopped

4 jalapeño or serrano chiles, stemmed and chopped (not seeded)

¼ cup chopped cilantro or flat-leaf parsley

1 lime, juiced

1 teaspoon kosher salt

6 grinds of black pepper

1 teaspoon sugar if the tomatoes are acidic (optional)

1. Combine the tomatoes, onion, garlic, chiles, cilantro, lime juice, salt, and pepper in a bowl. Mix well. Taste and add the optional sugar if necessary.

2. Let the mixture rest for 30 minutes for the flavors to blend. Taste for seasoning and serve at room temperature.

Variation: Uncooked Jícama-Tomato Table Salsa

1 cup chopped jícama adds a slightly sweet crunch to the salsa. Serve it with any dish that needs a bit of something fresh alongside, such as saucy enchiladas.

Note: Instant uncooked table salsa is made with 2 chopped tomatoes, 2 chopped jalapeño chiles, and the juice of 1 lime, all whirled together in a blender. For more interest, add garlic, onion, fresh herbs, salt and pepper.

Basic Cooked Tomato Sauce
Salsa de Jitomate

As in southern Italian cooking, cooked tomato sauce is the basis for so many of Mexico's exceptional dishes and it's made with the same ingredients: ripe tomatoes, onions, garlic, and oregano, plus Mexico's special ingredient, chile. The sauce may also be used as a table salsa if you serve it at room temperature—be sure to add extra chiles because it must be spicier than this basic cooked sauce. Or, delete the fresh chiles and add 2 tablespoons puréed *Chiles Chipotles en Adobo* (page 44). Leftover sauce may be refrigerated for up to 3 days, or it may be frozen.

Yield: about 4 cups

1½ pounds red-ripe tomatoes or 1 twenty-eight-ounce can plum tomatoes, drained

1 large white onion, chopped

6 garlic cloves, peeled

4 red jalapeño or serrano chiles (unseeded), or green if red are unavailable, chopped

¼ cup chopped cilantro or flat-leaf parsley

2 Tablespoons dried Mexican oregano

1 teaspoon kosher salt

8 grinds of black pepper

1 or 2 Tablespoons sugar

1 Tablespoon vegetable oil

1. Roughly chop the tomatoes and put them in a processor or blender container. Add the onion, garlic, chiles, herbs, salt, pepper, and sugar. Blend. Stir down everything in the blender, scraping the sides, pulsing the machine and keeping a little texture—this is not a completely smooth sauce.

2. Heat the oil in a deep pot and add the blended ingredients. Bring to a boil and boil uncovered for 2 minutes, then reduce the heat and simmer for 15 minutes. Taste for seasoning. If the tomatoes are acidic, add an additional tablespoon of sugar and continue cooking for 3 minutes.

Variation: Toasted Tomato Sauce

When you insist on maximum flavor intensity, toast (page 28) the raw vegetables. Toast the tomatoes and put them in a plastic bag to sweat. When they are cool enough to handle, slip off their skins and core. Put the tomatoes in a blender. Quarter the onion, toast, then put in a blender. Toast the garlic, slip off the skins, and add to the blender. Toast the chiles, then stem and seed. Add to the blender. Add the herbs and seasonings. Blend. Continue with step 2, above.

Basic Uncooked Tomatillo Table Salsa
Salsa de Tomatillo Fresca

Basic green sauce, known as *salsa de tomatillo* or *salsa verde,* is equally as popular as red tomato sauce in Mexican cooking. Tomatillos look like small green tomatoes covered in papery husks. As with all fresh table salsas, fresh tomatillo salsa can be made extra spicy with the addition of more chiles—as they say, to taste. To maintain the bright green color, use only fresh green chiles because red or dried chiles turn the salsa brown. You'll find that the citrus taste of tomatillos matches especially well with any dish that's generally enhanced with a squirt of lime.

Yield: about 2 cups

10 tomatillos (about 1 pound), papery husks removed, washed of their sticky surfaces, and cored

1 medium white onion, coarsely chopped

3 jalapeño or serrano chiles, stemmed and coarsely chopped (seeded if you want milder salsa)

8 cilantro sprigs, chopped

½ teaspoon kosher salt

8 grinds of black pepper

1. Bring salted water to a boil. Drop in the tomatillos and boil for 1 minute. Do not overcook. Drain and chop.

2. Place the tomatillos, onion, chiles, cilantro, salt, and pepper in a blender container. Blend to a coarse purée. Taste for seasoning and serve at room temperature within 3 hours.

Variation: Creamy Tomatillo and Avocado Table Salsa
Peel and pit 1 ripe Hass avocado and scoop the flesh into the blender with the room-temperature tomatillo salsa. Blend for a few seconds, keeping some texture.

TOMATILLOS

Basic Cooked Tomatillo Sauce
Salsa de Tomatillo

As with Basic Cooked Tomato Sauce (page 32), you may use tomatillo sauce as a table salsa when cooled and served at room temperature. Be sure to use a few extra chiles; it must be spicy. If you want to use dried chiles for a different flavor, remember that the color changes from green to terracotta. Tomatillo salsa is poured over enchiladas, tamales with their husks removed, and *chilaquiles* (before baking), to name a few dishes. Another idea, with either red or green sauce, is to add hot Vegetable Broth (page 90) and turn it into a delicious soup. The sauce may be refrigerated for up to 5 days or it may be frozen.
Yield: about 6 cups

1½ pounds (about 18) tomatillos, husks removed, washed and cored

5 jalapeño or serrano chiles, stemmed

1 large white onion, chopped

8 garlic cloves, chopped

3 fresh *epazote* sprigs, or ¼ cup chopped cilantro

1 Tablespoon kosher salt

8 grinds of black pepper

1 Tablespoon vegetable oil

3 cups Vegetable Broth (page 90) or thin vegetable bouillon

1. Bring salted water to a boil. Drop in the tomatillos and chiles and boil for 3 minutes.

2. Place the tomatillos, chiles, onion, garlic, *epazote* or cilantro, salt, and pepper in a blender container. Blend to a coarse purée.

3. Heat the oil in a deep pot. Pour in the sauce all at once, stirring for 5 minutes until it becomes a darker color. Pour in the broth and simmer for 30 minutes, until the sauce thickens. Taste for seasoning.

Variation: Basic Toasted and Cooked Tomatillo Sauce

Toasting brings out flavor from all Mexican vegetables—this recipe is the most delicious version of green sauce, bar none.

1. Husk, wash, core, and toast (page 28) the tomatillos and put in a blender container (never peel tomatillos). Blend.

2. Quarter the onion and toast it. Toast the garlic, slip off their skins, and add to the blender. Toast the chiles and stem. Add to the blender. Add the *epazote* or cilantro, salt, and pepper. Blend.

3. Fry the sauce as in step 3, above.

Tomato, Potato, and Avocado Uncooked Table Salsa
Salsa Fresca con Jitomate, Papa, y Aguacate

Travelers know Santa Clara del Cobre, Michoacán, as Mexico's copper center and the place to buy huge copper cauldrons for carnitas or jam boiling, hand-hammered serving plates, and (recently) tin-lined pots. The dining room of Hotel Camino Real (not related to the huge chain) offers a chunky table salsa packed with the region's specialty, avocados, and its delicious potatoes. Diced red or white potatoes cut the heat, so keep the seeds in your chiles. Diced avocados provide bites of the fruit's creaminess without the rich texture of mashed guacamole.

Yield: about 4 cups

1 white- or red-skinned potato, about 3 inches, quartered

2 avocados, ripe but still firm

4 red-ripe plum tomatoes, juiced and chopped

1 medium white onion, chopped

6 serrano chiles, stemmed and chopped

¼ cup chopped cilantro

2 teaspoons kosher salt

6 grinds of black pepper

1 lime, juiced

1. Bring water to a boil in a saucepan and add the potato. Cook until tender, about 15 minutes. Drain and cool the potato to room temperature. Peel and dice into ¼-inch pieces. Put into a bowl.

2. Cut the avocado in half, lengthwise, and separate the two sides. Remove the large pit by hitting it with the blade of a large knife, then wiggle the pit free and pull it off the knife with a towel. Peel the skin from both halves and dice the avocado the same size as the potato. Add it to the bowl with the potato.

3. Add the tomato, onion, chiles, cilantro, salt, pepper, and lime juice to the bowl and gently mix. Taste and adjust the seasoning. Serve at room temperature or slightly cool.

MARÍA LUISA VILLASEÑOR'S

Peanut-Tomato Uncooked Table Salsa
Salsa de Cacahuate y Jitomate

El Ten Ten Pie (meaning "a little something to keep you on your feet") is a tiny taco restaurant in San Miguel de Allende at the corner of Cuadrante and Cuna de Allende. All María's tacos are indeed tasty tidbits, but her salsas make those tacos positively come alive. A favorite with locals and tourists is her tomato-peanut table salsa. Try this versatile salsa as a dipping sauce for cold jícama spears or spooned over anything from rice to grilled vegetables and quesadillas, or simply dig in with a bag of purchased tortilla chips.

Yield: 1 cup

¼ cup dry-roasted peanuts, unsalted

6 unpeeled garlic cloves, toasted

4 de árbol chiles, stemmed, seeded, and toasted

5 plum tomatoes, toasted

½ teaspoon kosher salt

3 grinds of black pepper

1 teaspoon dried Mexican oregano

1. Place the peanuts, garlic, and crumbled chile in a blender and blend, turning the machine on and off and scraping down the sides with a rubber spatula. Add a few tablespoons of water to make blending possible.

2. Add the tomatoes (with blackened skins), salt, pepper, and oregano and purée. Let the flavors mingle for 30 minutes before serving at room temperature.

PEANUTS

Toasted Ancho Chile and Garlic Uncooked Table Salsa
Salsa Chimichurri

El Tejaban is a casual country restaurant high up in the remote mountains of Michoacán, on the outskirts and just west of Tacambero. The picture windows open to the air offer nonstop vistas of volcanic mountain ranges cascading as far as the eye can see. Cooking is done in the open on a wood-burning grill. El Tejaban's scrumptious appetizers are perfect receptacles for their olive-oil–based salsa chimichurri, which is placed on every table.

Yield: about 1½ cups

4 ancho chiles

12 garlic cloves, unpeeled

**1 medium white onion,
    unpeeled and quartered**

1 teaspoon kosher salt

4 grinds of black pepper

1 cup olive oil

1. Stem the chiles (keep seeds). Open the chiles flat and toast (page 28) just until they change color. Toast the seeds. Tear the chiles into pieces and put them in a blender container with the seeds.

2. Toast the garlic and onion, then peel the blackened skins. Place the garlic, onion, salt, and pepper in a blender. Add the oil and blend. Pour into a bowl and add a small spoon, because the oil separates and needs to be stirred when served.

GARLIC CLOVES

MARCELA LÓPEZ BRUN'S

Fresh Tropical Fruit Uncooked Table Salsa
Salsa Fresca de Fruta

Chunky fruit salsas are generally thought of as contemporary Southwestern concoctions, even though fresh fruit chutneys have been an Indian staple—and salsas a Mexican standby—for centuries. Marcela, a Puebla art dealer proud of her Indian tribal chief ancestor, loves to serve this salsa with rich *moles* or atop *sopes*. She says to experiment with the fruit—pears, cantaloupes, or nectarines are less exotic and equally delicious when tropical lovelies are out of season. Choose a chile color that best complements the fruit mixture: green, yellow, or orange. Because habaneros match so well with tropical fruits, the chiles are the reason fruit salsas are sensational on the Yucatán peninsula.

Yield: 2 cups

1 red or other mild onion

1 cup finely chopped mamey, papaya, mango, pineapple, zapote, or combination

4 chopped *epazote* leaves, or ¼ cup chopped cilantro

¼ habanero chile (you can always add more later but start with a small piece), stemmed, seeded, and finely chopped, or 3 chopped green or red jalapeños

¼ cup orange juice

1 lime, juiced

½ teaspoon kosher salt

1. Thickly slice the red onion and put the slices in a small bowl of cold water. Soak for 10 minutes (soaking makes the mild onion even milder) and dry.

2. Finely chop the onion and put in a bowl. Add the fruit, *epazote*, chile, juices, and salt. Mix well. Taste for seasonings and spiciness. Let the flavors mingle for 30 minutes before serving.

MAMEY

Neon-Orange Liquid-Fire Salsa
Salsa Chile Habanero

A popular Yucatecan bottled hot sauce is made with carrots and orange habanero chiles, which accounts for its fiery neon color. This easy, homemade version reaches new heights of spicy fury. Salsa chile habanero clenches the prize for hotness because the chile mixture is raw—it never touches the heat, which softens fresh ingredients. Or, for a slightly mellower version, cook the sauce and bottle it for later use. Let your conscience be your guide when it comes to the amount of habaneros you blend into the sweet juice.

Yield: about 1½ cups

1 cup freshly squeezed carrot juice (not canned); if you don't have a juicer, buy freshly squeezed carrot juice at a health food store

2 Tablespoons fresh lime juice

2 Tablespoons white vinegar

3 Tablespoons chopped onion

2 Tablespoons chopped garlic

3 orange or yellow habanero chiles, or to taste (green chiles turn the sauce brown), stemmed

1 teaspoon kosher salt

1 Tablespoon vegetable oil (for preserving only)

1. Put all the ingredients in a blender or processor and purée until completely smooth. If the sauce is too thick, add more carrot juice or water so the consistency resembles heavy cream. Strain into a serving bowl.

2. The salsa keeps fresh for only 2 days, covered and refrigerated.

Note: To preserve the salsa:

1. Heat the oil and pour in the sauce. Bring to a boil, reduce the heat, and cook for 20 minutes.

2. Sterilize enough small canning jars and their lids for the quantity of salsa you make (you may double or triple the recipe). Sterilize by boiling jars in water for 15 minutes. Turn off the heat and let the jars stand in the water.

3. Just before the jars are to be filled, invert them onto a kitchen towel to dry. Fill the jars while they are still hot.

4. Fill the jars and seal immediately. Invert, and cool to room temperature.

HABANERO CHILE

Spicy-Sweet Pepita-Sesame Paste with Chipotle Chiles, Plantains, and Apple Cider
Pipián de Puebla

Pipián is one of Mexico's great culinary gifts to the world. Pre-Hispanic nut pastes are thinned with various liquids and turned into sauces. Señora González's perfumy *pipián* is from the northern region of the state of Puebla. The sweetness comes from apple cider (a specialty of the mountainous area) and ripe plantains. The smoky spice comes from chipotle chiles. It's a splendid dish spooned over rice and chunks of steamed vegetables—make it when a VIP is coming for dinner.

Yield: 8 servings

½ **pound unsalted, raw, shelled, green pumpkin seeds (pepitas)**

½ **pound white sesame seeds**

4 or 5 *chiles chipotles en adobo*

2 cups apple cider or juice

1 ripe (black) plantain, skinned and thickly sliced

2 teaspoons kosher salt

8 grinds of black pepper

4 cups Vegetable Broth (page 90) or water

1. Toast (page 28) the pepitas until lightly brown (they will pop and jump around in your skillet). Put them in a bowl. Toast the sesame seeds for about 10 seconds, turning constantly, until golden, and put them in the bowl with the pepitas.

2. Put half the mixed seeds in a blender or processor container with the chiles. Add 1 cup of the cider and blend. Scrape down the blender sides with a spatula and blend again, adding some water if necessary. Remove to a large pot. Add the other seeds to the blender with the plantain, salt, pepper, and remaining cup of cider. Blend and scrape down the blender sides with a spatula and blend again. Add to the paste in the pot.

3. Heat the seed paste over the lowest heat and simmer for 1 hour, stirring with a wooden spoon and adding as little water as possible.

4. To turn the paste into a sauce, add the vegetable broth or water. Simmer for 10 minutes. Taste for seasoning. The sauce should have the consistency of textured heavy cream.

Note: Pumpkin seed paste is the classic main ingredient in most *pipiáns*, but for an easy *pipián*, you can try various nut and seed pastes offered at health food stores. The combination of peanut butter and sesame (tahini) is delicious with canned *chiles chipotles en adobo* but even better with homemade *Chiles Chipotles en Adobo* (page 44). Thin with water or vegetable broth and don't include plantains or cider if you prefer a nonsweet *pipián*. Experiment—you can't go wrong.

MOLCAJETE

DOLORES GONZÁLEZ DE MOLENA'S

Ancho Chile Cooked Sauce
Salsa Enchilada

Simple ancho chile sauce requires no toasting before cooking. Dolores never toasts hers and neither does her mother or grandmother, nor did her great-grandmother, who were all born and brought up just east of Guadalajara. This salsa is made with easy-to-find dried ancho chiles with their superb fruity, slightly smoky, yet nonspicy, flavor. Try the smooth sauce with *Enchiladas* (page 66) or *Chilaquiles* (page 143 or 144).

Yield: 3½ cups

8 ancho chiles, stemmed
and seeded

6 garlic cloves, coarsely
chopped

5 plum tomatoes, coarsely
chopped

2 teaspoons kosher salt

6 grinds of black pepper

4 cups water

1. Put the chiles, garlic, tomatoes, salt, pepper, and water in a nonreactive pot. Bring to a boil, then lower the heat to medium and reduce the sauce for 30 minutes, uncovered. As with most chile-based sauces, don't breathe the steam—if you do, you'll cough like crazy from the fumes. Remove from the heat and cool for a few minutes before proceeding.

2. Pour the lumpy liquid into a blender or processor, in two batches. Purée, then pass through a strainer because this is a smooth sauce.

Chile Seasoning Paste and Mexican Barbecue Sauce
Adobo

Adobo is either a dry or vinegar-moistened seasoning rub that's massaged into vegetables and acts as a marinade before cooking—just as *adobo* was originally developed to preserve meats in the days before refrigeration. The chiles are flavorful but mild—spice is definitely not a component of most *adobos*. Add a de árbol chile or two to give it a kick. *Adobo* keeps for 2 weeks, refrigerated, in a tightly closed glass jar (the seasoning rub is the same idea as Yucatán's *recado* pastes). Dolores also told me that, alternatively, the paste is often thinned with melted butter in Jalisco and used as a basting sauce. *Piloncillo (panela)* adds sweetness to *adobo* and turns it into a Mexican barbeque sauce. Her mother's yams, steamed until they are almost done, cut into slices, and brushed with this paste thinned with melted butter and dark brown sugar before being slipped under a hot broiler, are incredible.

Yield: about 2 cups

3 guajillo chiles

3 ancho chiles

1 de árbol chile (optional)

1 small white onion, quartered

4 garlic cloves, unpeeled

1 teaspoon cumin seed

1 three-inch *canela* stick, or ½
teaspoon ground cinnamon

1 teaspoon dried Mexican
oregano

1 teaspoon kosher salt

6 grinds of black pepper

⅓ cup vinegar, plus extra

2 Tablespoons vegetable oil

1. Cut off the stem ends of the dried chiles, including the clumps of seeds. Slit each chile down one side and open out flat and toast (page 28). Tear into pieces and put in a blender or processor container. Blend.

2. Toast the onion and garlic. Slip the skins off the garlic and add them to the blender with the onions. Toast the cumin seed and *canela* stick for a few seconds, until their aromas are released, but do not burn (do not toast ground spices). Add to the blender. Add the oregano, salt, pepper, and vinegar. Purée until smooth.

3. Heat the oil in a deep pot. Add the sauce and stir over high heat until the color changes, about 5 minutes.

Spicy, Smoky Chile Paste
Chiles Chipotles en Adobo

Try making your own *chiles chipotles en adobo* rather than using a canned product, then purée the entire batch and spoon it into ice cube trays. Freeze, and when the paste is frozen, unmold the cubes into a plastic freezer bag. You don't have to open a can if you need only one chile. Plus, there's no superfluous tomato sauce filler as in canned. Of course, the chiles are no longer whole, but in most cases recipes call for them to be chopped or puréed before using. Substitute 1 slightly rounded tablespoon of the paste when a recipe calls for 1 chile. Add to your bean pot; use in pumpkin, squash, or, especially, cream soups; cooked or fresh tomato or tomatillo salsa; tamale flavorings; salad vinaigrette dressings; or lightly smear it on a roll when making a *Mollete* (page 68).

Yield: slightly more than 2 cups

4 ounces chipotle chiles (chile size doesn't matter)

4 ancho chiles

8 garlic cloves, unpeeled

1 four-inch *canela* stick, or ½ teaspoon ground cinnamon

2 bay leaves

½ teaspoon cumin seed

2 teaspoons dried Mexican oregano

1 teaspoon dried thyme

2 Tablespoons vegetable oil

½ cup cider vinegar

2 Tablespoons *piloncillo (panela)* or dark brown sugar

2 teaspooons kosher salt

1. On a hot *comal,* toast the chiles. Boil, then soak them in a saucepan of boiled water for 30 minutes, or until soft. Remove and discard any stems, but not the seeds. Purée the chiles in a blender container with a few tablespoons of water.
2. Toast the garlic cloves. Slip off the skins and put the garlic in the blender. Toast the *canela* stick, break it up, and add it to the blender. Toast the bay leaves, then the cumin seed for a few seconds, and add to the blender. Blend.
3. Add the oregano and thyme. Blend the mixture until mostly smooth. Slowly add 1 cup of the chile soaking water during the blending. Be forewarned: You'll cough like crazy if you breathe the fumes directly.
4. Heat the oil in a deep pot. Scrape the chile purée into the pot and fry the thick sauce for about 3 minutes, stirring to keep the paste from sticking to the bottom. Add the vinegar, sugar, and salt. Reduce the heat and simmer, uncovered, for 30 minutes. Stir every 5 minutes or so. Cool. Store the paste in the refrigerator for months, or freeze as directed above.

Oaxacan Mild Red Mole
Mole Coloradito

Traditional *mole* recipes usually have ingredients lists a kilometer long and scare off most people before they get to the first step. This typical home recipe from Oaxaca is a simple version of the state's chile and tomato classic. María Elana's children enjoy the non-spicy *mole* because they find Oaxaca's famous black *mole* too pungent—its grownup taste comes from black chiles with their seeds and stems toasted to black. Experiment as all good Oaxacan cooks do: Add more fruit or brown sugar as sweeteners, or maybe ground *canela* or allspice to your taste. If you'd like more heat, add spicy chiles such as pequín or de árbol. Spoon *mole* over steamed or grilled vegetables sprinkled with toasted sesame seeds, plenty of rice, and warm corn tortillas (flour tortillas are unheard of with southern Mexican sauces). *Yield: 6 servings*

8 ancho chiles

8 guajillo chiles

½ cup raisins

8 garlic cloves, unpeeled

1 large white onion, quartered

½ cup shelled almonds

6 red-ripe plum tomatoes

1 teaspoon kosher salt

6 grinds of black pepper

3 Tablespoons vegetable oil

½ to 1 Mexican chocolate tablet

3 cups Vegetable Broth (page 90) or water

1. Cut off the stem along with the clump of seeds just under the stem of each chile. Open the chiles out flat by cutting them open vertically, then remove the stems and seeds.

2. Toast (page 28) the chiles on both sides. Put the chiles in a bowl. Add the raisins, cover with boiling water, and soak for 20 minutes.

3. Toast and peel the garlic cloves and the onion. Toast the almonds. Add to a blender container. Drain the chiles and raisins and put them in the blender. Blend, adding a few tablespoons of water as needed.

4. Toast and peel the tomatoes. Put them in the blender with the salt and pepper and purée until smooth.

5. Heat the oil to very hot in a deep pot. Add the blender ingredients and fry the sauce, stirring for 5 minutes. Add the ½ chocolate tablet and reduce the heat. Add the broth and simmer for 30 minutes, uncovered. Taste for seasoning. If you'd like a sweeter, stronger chocolate taste, add another ½ tablet and simmer until melted.

Yellow Mole with Vegetables
Mole Amarillo

Oaxaca's soupy *amarillo* is made with esoteric local chiles not readily seen, even in other regions of Mexico. The subtle flavor difference between *amarillo* made with those chiles and *amarillo* made with easy-to-find guajillo chile is apparent if you're Oaxacan, or tasting the *amarillos* side-by-side. Whether you make a bowl of *amarillo* in southern Mexico or in your home kitchen, the flavor will be more glorious and different than anything you can get at Tex-Mex border-style food joints.

Yield: 10 servings

For the sauce:

15 guajillo chiles

2 whole allspice

2 whole cloves

1 rounded Tablespoon cumin
   seed

1 rounded Tablespoon dried
   oregano

8 garlic cloves

2 small tomatoes, halved

2 Tablespoons vegetable oil

1. Heat a griddle or heavy skillet to very hot and cook the chiles for 10 seconds only to soften, not to toast. Rinse the chiles and put them in a saucepan with 2 cups water. Bring to a boil and cook for 2 minutes.

2. Put the chiles in a blender container with the allspice, cloves, cumin, oregano, and garlic and blend with the top askew covered with a kitchen towel (or the heat will blow it off). Add the chile cooking water and blend. Add the tomatoes and blend again.

3. Heat the oil in a saucepan. Press a third of the sauce through a strainer into the hot oil and cook, stirring. Press another third, then the remainder, adding a little hot water if necessary to get the sauce through. Reduce the heat and simmer the smooth sauce for 10 minutes.

**For the vegetables (substitute
   at will):**

2 pounds red potatoes,
   quartered

2 pounds carrots, peeled and
   sliced

1. Bring 3 quarts water to a boil. Add the potatoes and carrots. Cook for 10 minutes. Add the beans, corn, and *hoja santa,* avocado leaves, or cilantro. Boil for 5 minutes longer.

2. In a bowl, mix the 3 cups water into the *masa,* a little at a time, until it's all incorporated. Slowly pour the thinned *masa* into the boiling vegetable-chile water and stir well.

2 pounds green beans, cut into 2-inch pieces, or cactus paddles, trimmed and cut into ¼ x 2-inch pieces

4 ears of corn, each cut into 2-inch pieces

2 Tablespoons dried and crushed *hoja santa* leaves, 6 whole avocado leaves, or 1 tied bunch (about 20) fresh cilantro stems

½ pound *masa* (about 1 cup), made with *masa harina*

3 cups water

Add 3 cups more water. Cook for 10 minutes to thicken. Combine the sauce and vegetables. Serve *amarillo* in wide, shallow bowls and pass plenty of warm corn tortillas.

CORN ON THE COB

Green Mole Made from Vegetables, Seeds, and Herbs

Mole Verde de Pipián

The state of Puebla specializes in scrumptious *moles*—including world-famous *mole poblano,* made with chiles, nuts, seeds, and chocolate. The Aztec word *mole* means mixture or sauce, and all *moles* are precisely that—rich sauces made from a mixture of many ingredients but usually containing chiles, nuts, seeds, and vegetables. This *mole,* from Juanita's home in Tehuacán, the bottled-water capital of Mexico, is green from pumpkin seeds, fresh chiles, and tomatillos. *Moles* are poured over all sorts of vegetable, bean, and rice dishes, and are fabulous over grilled eggplant, squash, and yam slices. Serve with tortillas. *Yield: 6 servings*

6 poblano chiles

1 pound tomatillos

4 jalapeño chiles, stemmed, with seeds intact

1 white onion, quartered

4 garlic cloves

2 Tablespoons vegetable oil

½ pound unsalted, raw, shelled, green pumpkin seeds (pepitas)

¼ cup chopped walnuts or pecans

¼ cup chopped almonds

2 cups Vegetable Broth (page 90) or water

2 teaspoons kosher salt

6 grinds of black pepper

1. Toast (page 28) the poblano chiles, then sweat them in a plastic bag. Peel, stem, and remove the seeds. Put the chiles in a blender container.

2. Remove the papery husks from the tomatillos and wash to remove the sticky coating. Toast the tomatillos and the chiles and put them in the blender. Toast the onion and garlic and put them in the blender. Blend.

3. Heat 1 tablespoon of the oil in a large pot. Pour in the blender ingredients and fry the sauce, stirring, for 1 minute. Reduce the heat and simmer for 10 minutes.

4. Toast the pepitas (they will jump around and pop). Put them in the blender. Toast the nuts. Blend them with the pepitas and ½ cup water.

5. In a large heavy pot, heat the remaining tablespoon of oil. Add the seed-nut paste and fry the paste, stirring, for 30 seconds. Turn the heat down to simmer. Add the tomatillo mixture. Add the broth, salt, and pepper. Cook until all the broth is incorporated and the sauce is slightly thickened, about 20 minutes. Taste carefully and adjust seasonings.

AMALIA RULFO DE FERNÁNDEZ'S

Slightly Sour, Thick Cream
Crema

Crema, Mexico's version of France's crème fraîche and a close cousin to our sour cream, is a natural heat-neutralizer with hot chiles. A dollop of thick, slightly sour cream is beloved with salsas containing copious quantities of fire from Yucatan's habanero, Michoacán's perón (a.k.a. manzano), and Veracruz's chipotle, or the whole lineup of tiny incendiaries such as pequín, de árbol, and serrano seco chiles. As with crème fraîche, *crema* is a cultured (not acidified) dairy product that's made from thick, full-fat cream. U.S. sour cream is not full-fat, and contains stabilizers to keep the mixture from separating. Sour cream can't be boiled because it curdles, so heat this *crema* recipe to no more than a simmer when preparing recipes.

Yield: 2 *cups*

1 cup extra heavy (whipping) cream

1 cup sour cream, very fresh (check the date on the container)

1. Combine the heavy cream with sour cream in a jar. Seal the lid and let the cream sit at room temperature for 3 to 4 hours. The cream will thicken.

2. Refrigerate for up to 1 week. The exact taste, texture, and thickness of the *crema* will be determined by the quality and age of the creams used.

Note: Low-fat *crema* doesn't exist. You may try to substitute low-fat or nonfat sour cream or low-fat or nonfat yogurt in recipes, and heat to no more than a simmer.

Snacks

LIGHT MEXICAN SNACK FOODS ARE CALLED *BOTANAS*. THEY ARE tidbits to munch with margaritas, sangrítas, and tequila shooters, the equivalent of our potato chips and pretzels. A couple of Mexican favorites include *Taquitos* for salsa and guacamole dipping, and Salted Peanuts with Garlic and Chile. Bottoms up and pass the chips.

Antojitos are Mexican fun foods—most often prepared with *masa* or tortillas. These snacks are eaten outside the home: from street carts or from stand-up windows at fast food places. Tacos are *antojitos*. Mexicans don't consider a taco a meal—to them a taco is a quick bite when you need something to tide you over until the next repast. *Tacos, gorditas, enchiladas, sopes, huaraches, quesadillas, taquitos, flautas, garnachas, empanadas, panuchos, salbutes, mamelas, memenas, burritos, chimichangas, chalupas* —and the list goes on—are names of some of the best-known *antojitos*. They can drive a traveler nuts because the same snack is known by different names, or one name is used to describe different concoctions. Danger prevails if you order an *antojito* sight-unseen! But who cares—each and every one is a masterwork of munchability.

Hot Tortilla Chips Sprinkled with Fresh Lime Juice and Salt
Totopos (or Tostaditos)

*T*otopos, also known as *tostaditos,* or simply, corn chips, are everyone's favorite snack food. Corn tortillas are stacked, then cut into pie-shaped wedges before they are fried to a crunchy crisp. While the chips are hot, splash with fresh lime juice, then sprinkle with kosher salt. Warm, homemade *totopos* are perfect dipping tools for guacamole and salsas—nothing out of a bag comes close. Use day-old tortillas for deep frying because they absorb less oil than fresh.

Yield: 4 servings

2 cups vegetable oil, for frying

12 corn tortillas

1 lime

2 Tablespoons kosher salt

1. Heat the oil to 375°F. Meanwhile, cut the tortillas by stacking 6 at a time and cutting through the pile into sixths or eighths, depending on the size of the tortillas.

2. Separate the piles and fry a handful at a time until crisp. Remove from the oil with a slotted spoon and drain on a double layer of paper towels.

3. Squirt with fresh lime juice and sprinkle with salt while hot. Continue with the remaining tortilla pieces, adding more lime and salt. Serve as hot as possible.

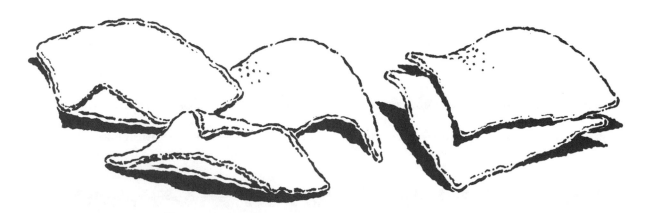

Roasted Chiles with Onions and Cream
Rajas con Crema

The word *rajas* is Spanish for "strips," and in Mexico's kitchens they're most often strips of fresh poblano chile. Regional chiles sparkle in Oaxaca's very spicy de agua chile *rajas,* Gulf coast Veracruz's largest jalapeño chiles are sliced for theirs, and the west coast states of Sinaloa and Nayarit enjoy *rajas* from their plentiful poblanos mixed with hard-to-find fresh guajillo chile. In the U.S., if you can't find poblano chiles, green, red, yellow, and gold bell peppers make mild yet delicious *rajas*—if you'd like some spice add green or red jalapeños or yellow wax chiles.

Toasted (page 28) *rajas* are stirred into caramelized onions and garlic to form the basis of endless authentic Mexican dishes. Add *crema* if you want a creamy filling for tacos, enchiladas, tamales, *sopes,* or similar *antojitos. Rajas con crema* make a radiant dip to scoop with homemade *Totopos* (page 52). Puréed *rajas* transform into soups and creamy sauces. *Yield: 2½ cups*

1 pound large poblano chiles (about 5)

1 Tablespoon vegetable oil

2 medium white onions, sliced on the diagonal

4 garlic cloves, finely chopped

1 cup Crema (page 49) or to taste), optional

Kosher salt and freshly ground black pepper to taste

1. Toast (page 28) and sweat the chiles. Stem, seed, and peel. Slice into vertical strips ¼ inch wide.

2. In a large skillet, heat the oil. Add the onion and sauté until golden. Add the garlic and cook another 2 minutes. Add the chiles and heat through.

3. Add the *crema* if desired. Season at this point with salt and pepper. Heat through and taste for seasoning.

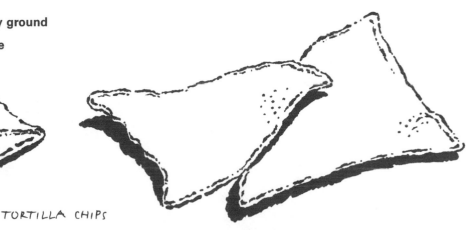

TORTILLA CHIPS

Tiny Potatoes with Caramelized Garlic
Papitas al Ajo

Mercedes, owner of Bugambilia restaurant (page 212), loves to serve these *botanas* in her home to favored guests. She slowly browns teeny boiled potatoes, then adds chopped garlic that has been half-cooked in olive oil (a Veracruzana touch) until deep gold, sticky, and chewy. She serves a bowl of these cocktail munchies speared with toothpicks. I adore the garlicky potatoes as a dinner side dish too, because no one has to stick his or her finger indelicately into the bowl to get more of the heavenly caramelized garlic. (Don't think it won't happen.)

Yield: about 12 servings with cocktails, 6 as a potato dish

2 pounds baby red or white potatoes, 1 inch maximum

¼ cup olive oil

½ cup coarsely chopped garlic

2 teaspoons kosher salt

8 grinds of black pepper

1 Tablespoon ancho chile powder, or 1 toasted, seeded, and pulverized ancho chile

½ cup finely chopped flat-leaf parsley

1 Tablespoon lime juice

1. Bring 3 quarts of salted water to boil and add the potatoes. Cook, cover askew, until done, about 20 minutes. Drain well then blot dry.

2. Heat the olive oil and add the potatoes. Sauté until lightly browned.

3. Add the garlic, lower the heat, and slowly simmer until the garlic turns dark golden and becomes carmelized. Remove the potatoes and garlic to a bowl. Add the salt, pepper, ancho chile powder, parsley, and lime juice. Mix well. Cool to serve slightly warm or at room temperature with round toothpicks.

Salted Peanuts with Garlic and Chile
Cacajuates con Ajo, Chile, y Sal

Cafés lining Oaxaca's main square offer a plate of these addictive warm tidbits when you place a drink order. Spicy, salty, red-skinned peanuts are mixed with a few browned garlic cloves. The cloves are about the same size and color as a peanut so your taste buds are jolted awake the first time you get one. Later, you'll hunt through the small pile of nuts until you find your prize. The peanuts can be spicy or mild depending on the type of chile powder you choose: ancho is slightly smoky and mild while de árbol or pequín will set your sinuses free. Whatever you choose, be sure the powder is pure and not blended with salt, paprika, and other fillers. Some people like to squirt fresh lime on the peanuts, so put a small bowl of lime wedges next to the bowl of nuts. Pass plenty of napkins.

Yield: about 2 cups

3 Tablespoons vegetable oil

2 garlic heads (about 24 cloves)

1 can (12 ounces) roasted, salted Spanish red-skinned peanuts

2 limes, quartered

1 Tablespoon pure chile powder (or to taste)

1. Preheat the oven to 350°F.

2. Heat the oil and garlic in a large skillet. Cook very slowly until the garlic turns dark golden to medium brown—absolutely do not blacken or the garlic will be bitter and you'll have to start all over again. Remove the garlic to a bowl with a slotted spoon.

3. Meanwhile, heat the peanuts on a baking sheet for about 5 minutes, until they are warm. Add to the bowl with the garlic and squirt with 1 lime wedge. Add the chile powder and mix well. Serve the remaining lime wedges in a separate small bowl next to the bowl of peanuts.

Variations: Salted Pepitas with Garlic and Chile, and Salted Popcorn with Garlic and Chile
The same method applies with pepitas (shelled pumpkin seeds). Toast raw seeds before adding the chile mixture. Buttered popcorn takes on another dimension with garlic, chile, and salt—but lime juice deflates popped corn.

PEPITAS AND PEANUTS

CARLOS JÉSUS LÓPEZ DE AGUILAR'S

Chile- and Lime-Splashed Jícama and Cucumber Spears

Jícama y Pepinos con Chile y Limón

Here's Mexican street food at its best. Vendors sell slices of cucumbers and jícama arranged in plastic cups from carts parked on street corners all over Mexico—just like at Carlos's cart encamped on a corner in Guadalajara. Carlos splashes peeled jícama and cucumber spears with fresh lime juice, then sprinkles them with pequín chile powder. The cold, refreshing, crunchy vegetables are a welcome relief on scorching summer days when fruit ices, juice, or even soda, seem too sweet.

Yield: 4 servings

2 cucumbers

1 jícama, about 4 inches in diameter

1 or 2 limes

1 Tablespoon chile powder

1 teaspoon kosher salt

1. Cut the ends off the cucumbers then peel (if you cut the ends off first, you cut away bitterness). Peel the jícama. Slice the cucumber into 8 vertical spears, keeping the seeds intact or not, as you like. Slice the jícama into spears about the same size as the cucumber.

2. Put half of the cucumber and jícama spears in each of 2 plastic cups (for authenticity) or arrange on a plate. Squirt lime juice generously over the vegetables and sprinkle with chile powder and salt to taste.

MEXICAN LIME WEDGES

ESTELA ARMAS DE RUIZ'S

Mashed Avocado Dip
Guacamole

The recipe for guacamole in *A Cook's Tour of Mexico* remains my favorite. There's no match to the clean taste of buttery Hass (previously spelled Haas) avocado mashed with lime juice and nothing else. Over-spiced and over-enhanced guacamole is almost as bad as guacamole blended to a smooth purée. Keep it simple. Keep the lumps. Pass a spicy table salsa and tortilla chips.

Yield: 6 servings

2 or 3 (depending on size) black-ripe and soft Hass avocados

1 lime, juiced

1. Cut the avocados in half, remove the pits, and scoop the flesh into a bowl.

2. With a fork, mash the avocado so it's a bit lumpy—not a purée. Add the lime juice and mix lightly. Salt is unnecessary because corn chips have plenty. If you're dipping with vegetables, add salt to taste.

AVOCADO

Chipotle Chile-Sour Cream Dip
Crema con Chile Chipotle

If you want something other than guacamole for a fiesta, here's a new twist on the old sour cream party dip. One day when Dora made me a super-simple sandwich spread in her Chiapas kitchen from canned chipotle chiles ground into *crema,* I mentioned to her that it would make a dynamite dip. She confessed she had never prepared the spread as a dip, in fact, she didn't know what one was. I taught her the ropes—we first cut a pile of raw veggies into finger food, then dunked the vegetables into her sandwich spread. Dora wanted more heat, so mincing another chile and adding it at the end was no problem. Since sour cream can now be purchased low-fat and fat-free, adding chipotles turns this simple combo into a guiltless flavor explosion.

Yield: 2 cups

3 canned *chiles chipotle en adobo* (or to taste)

1 pint Crema (page 49) or sour cream (full-, low-, or nonfat)

1. Put the chiles in a blender container. Blend.

2. Add a big spoonful of *crema* or sour cream and blend until the chile is completely puréed. Using a spatula, scrape the chile mixture into the remaining *crema.* Mix thoroughly. Taste. Add another puréed chile if you want more spice.

Variations: To turn the dip into a spread, add puréed chipotle chiles to whipped cream cheese, then put it into a small bowl and serve with crackers. Chipotle-enhanced low-fat mayonnaise boosts most sandwiches and veggie burgers to new taste plateaus.

Tacos

Nothing is more simple, more scrumptious, or more Mexican than a taco. When a warm corn tortilla envelops almost any food it becomes Mexico's favorite *antojito,* a taco. Those deep-fried, U-shaped tortillas housing ground meat, shredded American cheese, and iceberg lettuce are far from what you'll encounter in Mexico. Authentic tacos are based on a double thickness of small, heavenly scented warm corn tortillas with something grilled, griddled, or stewed on top, then hit with a squirt of lime and bottled hot sauce. Both tortillas are picked up at once, folded, and bitten into super-pronto. It's street-food perfection eaten with the juices dripping onto a sidewalk already splattered with juice from other tacos that are but memories.

Yield: 1 taco

2 small corn tortillas, no larger than 5 inches
¼ cup taco ingredients (see suggestions below)
Table salsa and/or bottled hot sauce
Lime wedges

1. Heat a nonstick skillet to hot. Lay 2 tortillas in the skillet for 10 seconds, turn over, and heat for another 10 seconds. Slightly overlap the 2 tortillas on a plate.

2. Top the tortillas with a big spoonful of any interesting concoction (including chopped leftovers). If the tortillas are large, say 6 inches, one is enough per taco. Pass hot sauce, of course, and fresh lime wedges.

Filling suggestions: *Tacos de cazuela* are tortillas topped with long-simmered stewlike concoctions. Equally revered are skillet-sautéed treats such as *Rajas* (page 53) or scrambled eggs cooked with *rajas;* Mexican-style home fries with chiles and cilantro; mushrooms or, for that matter, any vegetable sautéed with onions and chiles, or sauced with a luscious *mole;* cooked vegetables mixed with chile-illuminated *Pipián* (page 40); refried or puréed beans topped with radish slices and chopped onion; or cold vegetable *Escabeche* (page 106) with avocado slices and a sprinkle of a *queso fresco* such as ranchero cheese, are but a mouthful of suggestions.

Masa Tartlets with Scrumptious Fillings
Sopes

Sopes are small, thick corn dough pancakes with turned-up edges resembling tiny tarts. They're topped with mouth-watering fillings and piled with shredded greens. *Sopes,* also called *guarnachas, picadas,* and *chalupas,* among other names depending on the region of Mexico, can be anywhere from 5-inch circles to 1½-inch *botanas* for cocktail fare. They are either round or made boat-shaped by pinching 2 opposite sides. Large *sopes* are cooked on an ungreased griddle; tiny *sopes* are deep-fried. Marcela serves these *sopes* with her Fresh Tropical Fruit Uncooked Table Salsa (page 38), or try a drizzle of *Salsa Chimichurri* (page 37), a toasted ancho chile and garlic masterpiece from Michoacán.
Yield: 25 sopes, about 2½ inches each

2 pounds *masa* from a tortillería, or 4 cups *masa harina* mixed with 2¼ cups water and 1 teaspoon kosher salt

2 cups vegetable oil for frying

1. Pull off golf ball–sized pieces and form 25 balls. Flatten each ball into a 3-inch disk. Place on a baking sheet and cover with plastic wrap to keep from drying out while you finish the remaining disks.

2. Heat the oven to 400°F. Heat an ungreased *comal,* griddle, or large skillet and cook a few disks for about 3 minutes. Turn over and brown the other sides. Quickly pinch up the sides ¼ inch while the disks are hot and pliable (hot fingertips are a hazard). Place on a baking sheet while finishing the rest. Reheat in the oven.

3. Fill and garnish with suggestions below or devise an exciting concoction of your own.

Filling suggestions: Refried pinto beans with shredded cheese, shredded cabbage, and a few radish slices; baked eggplant mashed with chipotle chiles; black beans with *epazote,* topped with chunky uncooked tomato salsa; guacamole with vinegared red onions; or corn kernels with tomatillo salsa topped with ranchero cheese and shredded iceberg lettuce.

Cheese-Filled Tortilla Turnovers
Quesadillas de Queso

Quesadillas are one of the easiest *antojitos* to prepare and one of the most appealing. They're so popular in the U.S. that quesadillas can be found on school cafeteria lunch menus as well as on the menu at good old Jack-in-the-Box. Quesadillas run the gamut from melted cheese in a folded tortilla to elaborate Fusion-New Wave-Pacific Rim concoctions served in trendy restaurants. They are deep-fried, panfried, and griddle-cooked. Homemade tortillas are undeniably superior to anything purchased, but you'll be forgiven if yours are store bought. Quesadillas can also be low-fat: Use low-fat cheese (one that melts), and a few chile strips, and cook them in a nonstick pan. Serve with an oil-free, uncooked table salsa.
Yield: 1 cheese quesadilla

1 teaspoon vegetable oil

1 corn or flour tortilla

⅓ cup shredded quesillo de Oaxaca, mozzarella, or Monterey Jack cheese

1 chile, either a pickled jalapeño or a toasted, seeded, and peeled poblano (optional), sliced into strips

1. Lightly oil a griddle or skillet and heat to medium. Lay a tortilla on the hot surface and heat for 10 seconds. Flip over and sprinkle with the cheese.

2. When the cheese begins to melt (about 1 minute), arrange the chile on top. Fold the tortilla in half and continue cooking until crisp, flipping it a few times. Cut into 3 or 4 pie-shaped pieces and serve piping hot with salsa.

Variations: Before folding the tortilla in half, top the melting cheese with: caramelized onions and garlic; *Rajas* (page 53); sautéed mushrooms; squash blossoms; *epazote* leaves; bean purée, or any great Mexican mixture you can devise. New Wave restaurant specimens such as French chèvre with chanterelle mushrooms, Gorgonzola with pears, and white truffled fontina cheese all have humble roots—they are direct descendants of modest cheese quesadillas.

Exotic Corn Mushroom Tortilla Turnovers
Quesadillas de Huitlacoche

Angelika moved to Mexico in 1979 from her native Berlin after roaming around the U.S. and Canada searching for her place in the sun. She settled in San Miguel de Allende and opened her patio restaurant, El Meson de San José (page 213). She offers delicious *huitlacoche* quesadillas every summer when the corn fungus materializes in the markets during Mexico's rainy season. In the morning at the Tuesday open-air market, you'll spot velvety gray growths on ears of corn still in their leaves. *Huitlacoche* sells out fast. By noon, the local gourmets have snatched up any choice specimens. *Huitlacoche* is an exotic mushroomlike fungus; its texture and rich flavor are truly indescribable but definitely herbal, earthy, slightly smoky, and touched with the scent of morel mushroom. It can inspire you to take a trip to Mexico's mountainous regions during the summer for a first-hand taste. In the weekly markets where Indians sell their bounty, look for mushrooms that are mostly pale gray with a velvet texture; when they turn shiny black, *huitlacoche* is past its prime (even though it turns dark when cooked). Fresh and frozen *huitlacoche* are available (see Mail-Order Sources, page 204); use the Mexican canned product as a last resort.

Yield: 6 servings, 2 quesadillas each

4 ears of corn filled with
   huitlacoche

1 Tablespoon butter

1 onion, finely chopped

2 garlic cloves, finely chopped

½ teaspoon cumin seed

2 medium tomatoes, peeled,
   juiced, and finely chopped

1 teaspoon kosher salt

6 grinds of fresh pepper

12 small, thin, flour tortillas,
   6 inches in diameter

1. Remove the leaves and corn silk from the ears of corn and wash the *huitlacoche* well. Drain.

2. Heat the butter in a skillet and add the onion, cooking until it is transparent. Add the garlic and cumin and continue stirring until golden.

3. Add the tomatoes. Scrape the *huitlacoche* and any remaining corn kernels off the cobs and into the skillet. Add the salt and pepper. Turn down the heat and simmer the mixture for 10 minutes, or until the *huitlacoche* is soft.

4. Take a tortilla in one hand and spread 2 tablespoons shredded (Angelika charmingly calls it "ruffled") cheese over the surface. Spoon on a generous amount of *huitlacoche*

1½ cups shredded quesillo de Oaxaca, mozzarella, or Monterey Jack cheese

1 Tablespoon vegetable oil

mixture, fold to form a thick quesadilla, and put it on a very lightly oiled griddle or in a nonstick skillet. Cook for about 30 seconds, turn, and cook the other side only until the cheese melts; do not brown the tortillas. Continue with the other quesadillas.

Variation:

Huitlacoche Crepes

Since the days of French rule in Mexico, savory crepes (page 165, made without sugar) have been a special occasion food. *Huitlacoche* crepes are seen all summer in tony places from Guadalajara to Puebla. They're rolled or folded with filling inside, and topped with a spoonful of *Crema* (page 49).

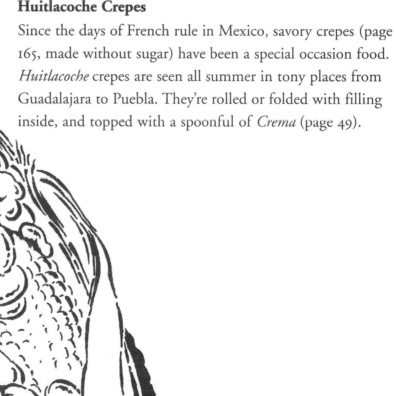

HUITLACOCHE

Beans and a Salad Piled on Fried Tortillas
Tostadas

Mexican tostadas are smaller and simpler than the fried flour tortilla monsters we see in pseudo-Mexican restaurants. Mexicans arrange corn (never flour) tortillas side-by-side on an oval plate. They're covered with a thin layer of refried beans, shredded cabbage or iceberg lettuce, and radish slices. A spoonful each of crumbled cheese, *crema,* and guacamole rounds everything out. Lime wedges and a fiery salsa are mandatory—try something different in the sauces chapter (page 27) or purchase a wicked bottled hot sauce.

Yield: 2 servings

¼ cup vegetable oil

4 small corn tortillas

1 cup refried or puréed beans

½ cup crumbled ranchero or
   mild feta cheese

2 cups shredded green
   cabbage or iceberg lettuce

4 radishes, sliced

1½ cups Crema (page 49), or
   sour cream

1½ cups Guacamole (page
   57), or a sliced avocado

1 lime, quartered

1. Heat the oil to hot. Carefully slip in a tortilla and fry until crisp. Drain on paper towels. Continue with the remaining tortillas.

2. Lay 2 fried tortillas on an oval (if possible) plate. Smear them with beans. Top with cheese, cabbage or lettuce, and radish slices. Spoon a dollop of *crema* and guacamole on top or on the side. Serve with lime wedges and salsa.

RADISHES

Stuffed, Tightly Rolled, and Fried Tortillas
Taquitos

Another fried tortilla-based *antojito* is the *taquito* (called a *cotzito* in Yucatán). A spoonful of filling is placed on a corn tortilla, then tightly rolled, secured with a toothpick, and deep-fried until golden brown and crackling crisp. Guacamole is the quintessential *taquito* dip—nobody said these munchables are for calorie watchers.

Yield: 12 taquitos

2 cups vegetable oil

1¼ cups filling (see below)

12 corn tortillas

1. Heat the vegetable oil to 375°F.

2. Spread 2 tablespoons filling on a tortilla, keeping it half an inch from the edge. Roll the tortilla tightly *(very* tightly) and secure with a round toothpick.

3. Fry a few *taquitos* at a time until each is crisp and deep golden brown. Drain on paper towels. Remove the toothpicks. Serve hot.

Filling suggestions: Any highly flavored mixture, because there's such a diminutive amount in each *taquito:* finely chopped grilled vegetables and serrano chiles bound with shredded cheese; chopped potatoes sautéed then simmered in a tomato-chile sauce; and fresh corn kernels with homemade *Chiles Chipotles en Adobo* (page 44).

Filled, Sauced, and Baked Tortillas
Enchiladas al Horno

Enchilada (chile) sauce is made all over Mexico. The flavor varies, depending on what regional dried chiles are used. Enchiladas in southern Mexico are simply corn tortillas that are first heated in hot oil, dipped in chile sauce, then folded twice and sprinkled with a smidgen of cheese. Northern-style, generously filled and baked enchiladas are an entirely different animal: Tortillas are first heated in hot oil and dipped in chile sauce before being stuffed, rolled, arranged in a dish, sauced, topped with cheese, and baked. Assemble them fast because enchiladas get mushy if you let them sit before baking. To look authentic, just like Francisca's gems from the northern state of Sinoloa, near Mazatlán, serve two enchiladas on each plate and decorate with shredded lettuce, tomato wedges, avocado slices, a few raw onion rings, and a radish rose.

Yield: 8 enchiladas (4 servings)

2 teaspoons vegetable oil

2 zucchini, halved lengthwise

1 ear of corn, husks removed

1 red bell pepper, quartered lengthwise and seeded

¾ cup shredded Monterey Jack cheese (low-fat if desired)

3 Tablespoons chopped cilantro

1 teaspoon kosher salt

8 grinds of black pepper

¼ cup vegetable oil

½ recipe Enchilada Sauce (page 42)

8 corn tortillas

¼ cup shredded ranchero or Monterey Jack cheese

1. Preheat the oven to 350°F and the grill to hot.

2. Grill lightly oiled (so they don't stick to the grill) zucchini, corn, and bell pepper. Cool enough to handle and scrape the kernels off the corn into a large bowl. Finely chop the zucchini and pepper the same size as the corn kernels and mix with the corn. Add the ¾ cup cheese, cilantro, salt, and pepper, and mix.

3. Heat ¼ cup oil in a small skillet. Put the sauce in a wide bowl. Spread ½ cup sauce in a baking dish that's just large enough for the enchiladas to fit snugly when rolled.

4. Dip a tortilla in the sauce. Place it in the hot oil for 3 seconds; turn over, and cook for 2 seconds. With tongs, carefully remove to a plate. Spoon about ¼ cup vegetable mixture in the center of the tortilla and roll. Place the enchilada seam side down in the baking dish. Continue with the remaining enchiladas. Sprinkle with the ¼ cup cheese. Bake for 5 minutes to melt the cheese.

Tortillas Filled with Black Bean Purée
Panuchos

Panuchos are adored by everyone on the Yucatán peninsula, especially at *fondas* in the Valladolid market. Pull up a stool to watch a woman split open a handmade tortilla and dexterously stuff it with *epazote* flavored black bean purée. Then she puts the filled tortilla on a *comal* and browns both sides. You choose whether to have toppings mounded on yours, or just a bit of vinegared red onion. Rosario says that *panuchos* are served instead of plain tortillas for special occasions at home. She says to try them with Vegetables Baked in Banana Leaves (page 138)—it's a traditional combination in the region between Mérida and Valladolid.

Yield: 8 panuchos

8 corn tortillas, on the thick side

1 cup refried black beans, seasoned with *epazote* (use cilantro if *epazote* is unavailable), and puréed in a blender

2 Tablespoons vegetable oil

2 habanero chiles, halved

1. Heat a tortilla on an ungreased *comal* or griddle.

2. Remove to a plate. With a knife, carefully cut a horizontal slit in the tortilla and form a pocket.

3. Spoon about ¼ cup beans into the pocket. Spread the purée around and flatten the tortilla with your fingers, being careful not to break the fragile tortilla layers. Repeat with the remaining tortillas.

4. Heat the oil in a skillet. Carefully lay a *panucho* in the hot oil for 20 seconds. Turn it over and cook until the tortilla bottom is lightly brown and crisp, about 1 minute. Remove from the oil and place on paper towels to drain. For authenticity, offer halved habanero chiles for people to gently and quickly wipe across their *panucho*—for flavor and spice.

HABANERO CHILE

Beans and Melted Cheese on French Rolls
Molletes

Molletes are standard market foods and quick snacks. They're cheap and filled with pro-tein. This is the time-honored way to prepare the sandwiches, yet many cooks toast the cut roll first, then smear beans on the cut sides before they add cheese and pop the two pieces under a broiler and serve them open-faced. Garnish with lettuce, slices of tomato, onion, radishes, pickled vegetables, or small pieces of canned *chiles chipotles en adobo.*

Yield: 2 sandwiches

2 *bolillos* or French rolls,
    about 3 x 6 inches

1 cup refried or puréed beans

½ cup shredded quesillo de
    Oaxaca, mozzarella, or
    Monterey Jack cheese
    (low-fat is fine)

1 Tablespoon vegetable oil

1. Cut the rolls in half, lengthwise. Generously slather the bottom halves with beans. Top with a layer of cheese. Cover with the top halves of the roll.

2. Heat the oil in a skillet. Cook just like a grilled cheese sandwich. Press down on the rolls with a spatula to flatten them a bit. Turn over and brown the other side. Be sure the cheese is melted before serving.

Filled and Rolled Flour Tortillas
Burritos

Burritos are always made with flour tortillas that are larger (10 to 12 inches in diameter) than standard 6-inch corn tortillas. The northern Mexican border states' specialty is most often filled with beef or pork mixtures, but meatless burritos are easy-to-eat packages enclosing a great heap of beans, rice, chopped cooked and raw vegetables, shredded cheese, scrambled or hard-boiled eggs, avocado slices, and chiles, whether fresh, pickled, or in a salsa.

Yield: 1 burrito

1 large flour tortilla

1 cup filling (or more,
    depending on tortilla size)

1. Heat a griddle or nonstick skillet and warm the tortilla—it must be warm and pliable or it will tear when rolled. Place the warm tortilla on a plate and generously top with at least 1 cup of a filling—mixtures are best.

2. Fold as you would a Chinese egg roll: Fold in the two end flaps then roll. To eat "to go" style: Wrap the bottom half in paper then pick it up with both hands and bite. Keep the burrito tightly rolled or the filling will fall out. For restaurant or home style: Place the burrito on a plate, seam side down, and cover with either Basic Cooked Tomato Sauce (page 32) or Basic Cooked Tomatillo Sauce (page 34).

Tamales

REMEMBER WHEN THE WORDS "HOT TAMALES" PROVOKED A twitching stomach and nervous smile? Tamales have become so popular in the U.S. that they're sneaking onto mainstream restaurant menus and into supermarket freezers. Now you relish a tamale's incredible corn perfume, full flavor, and exciting texture. Mexico's delicious tamales have been known as fiesta food since pre-Hispanic times when they were gifts to the gods during the twelfth month of the Mayan eighteen-month calendar year. Then the ancient Mayan fiesta days and new Spanish holiday, All Saint's Day, overlapped. Tamales became special food to be displayed on Day of the Dead altars to honor the dead. In Mexico today, any tamale fiesta begins with the actual tamale making, when a select group of friends gather to prepare hundreds of *masa*-filled, leaf-wrapped packages. Everyone gets a job, and the assembly line rolls.

Tamales made with Coarsely Ground Masa and Wrapped in Husks
Tamales Norteños

Tamales are made with *masa* (corn dough) bought at tortillerías. They are also prepared the modern way: with *masa* made with *masa harina* (treated corn flour purchased at supermarkets) and reconstituted with water. *Masa* is beaten with shortening until fluffy, then spread on aromatic leaves and topped with a filling. The leaves are folded and the packages steamed. Tamales made with coarse *masa* and wrapped in dried corn husks are the tamales of choice in northern Mexico.

The difference between corn dough for tortillas and corn dough for tamales is texture. Tortillas are made from finely ground corn dough so the delicate pancakes can be thinly pressed. Tamales are made with two *masa* grinds: Tamales wrapped in banana leaves (southern-style) are made with the same finely ground corn dough as tortillas. After they are steamed, the dough texture is smooth and delicate, similar to that of thick pasta. Tamales wrapped in corn husks (northern-style) are made with coarsely ground corn dough, so after the tamales steam, they have the fluffy, coarse texture of muffins. Traditional tamales have freshly rendered lard beaten into the dough for taste and fluffiness. Substitute butter. Vegetable shortening works fine, but add salsa or herbs to the shortening for great flavor. Also, a long mixing time ensures fluffy tamales. Tamales are just as heavenly refrigerated and reheated as they are fresh. They also freeze successfully. Reheat frozen tamales for about 20 minutes in a steamer. Leftovers, with wrappings removed, sliced and pan sautéed until crispy brown, are nothing short of one of life's small miracles.

Make tamales as spicy as you wish by the type of chile you add to the filling. Serve tamales with a hot table salsa and *Crema* (page 49).

Yield: about 25 medium tamales

For the corn husks:

1 8-ounce package dried corn husks (found in many supermarkets, Latino markets, or by mail order)

1. Remove the largest dried leaves and rinse. Don't open the centers of the husks or your sink will be full of corn silk. Cover the leaves with boiling water in a large pot and soak for 1 hour, or until they are pliable. Weight the leaves down with a water-filled bowl to keep them submerged.

2. Use only the largest leaves for wrapping tamales—there are more than enough in a package. Tear smaller leaves into strips to use as ribbons to tie tamales closed, if desired.

For the filling:

Prepare a filling before beginning the dough. The list is almost limitless—let your imagination run wild after you've tried a few basics such as a simple smear of *Adobo* (page 43). Fresh corn kernels are sensational with glazed onions for an easy, nonspicy filling; tomatillo salsa and cheese is classic; *nopales* or green beans and roasted garlic is extraordinary, with Mexican oregano mixed into the *masa*. Chopped grilled vegetables make a fabulous stuffing; a piece of Monterey Jack cheese and a strip of toasted fresh chile is another; chopped olives, capers, raisins, and chipotle chile salsa; black beans seasoned with *hoja santa* or *epazote;* toasted chile strips and garlic slices caramelized in olive oil; or sautéed wild mushrooms with Basic Cooked Tomatillo Salsa (page 34) are a few suggestions.

For the dough:

1⅓ cups butter or vegetable shortening

2 pounds (about 4 cups) coarsely ground *masa* from a tortillería (not *masa preparada* because it has fat incorporated), or *masa* made from 4 cups coarse *masa harina* and 4 cups Vegetable Broth (page 90) or

1. Whip the butter or vegetable shortening until it is fluffy and aerated, 5 minutes with a mixer, three times as long by hand with fast folding motions.

2. Add the *masa,* a handful at a time, with the baking powder, oregano, and salt. Mix well and continue to mix. If the mixture becomes too thick, add up to ½ cup tepid broth or water. This step takes at least 10 minutes; you will feel the *masa* become light and fluffy with a spongy texture. The prepared *masa* is now ready to be spread onto leaves and topped with a filling.

(Continued)

warm water (2 pounds *masa*
makes about 25 medium-
sized tamales)

2 teaspoons baking powder

3 Tablespoons dried Mexican
oregano

1 Tablespoon kosher salt

To assemble:

1. Place a large, soaked husk on the table (sides curling inward) and, with a spatula, smear ¼ to ⅓ cup *masa* over the wide end from side to side and about halfway to the pointed end. Many people "glue" 2 husks together with a smear of *masa* to increase the tamale size. (Hey, it's okay to be messy—they'll still be delicious.)

2. Place a generous tablespoon of filling in the center of the *masa* toward the wide end. Fold the right edge over to the center, then roll toward the left third. Flap the narrow end over to the wide end, leaving the end open (this is the easiest tamale-making system). For other tamale shapes, you may tie the middle, end (or ends, depending on the shape you choose) with ribbons of husk from the smaller soaked leaves cut into ¼-inch strips. For an envelope shape: Place *masa* and filling on the center of a husk, leaving the edges clean; fold the right side to the center, then the left side to the center; fold each end to the center, overlapping, and tie with a husk ribbon around the middle. Rolled tamales look good: Spread the *masa* and filling in the center of a husk, then roll up the long way. Tie both ends. Place finished tamales in a bowl, open ends up, until ready to steam.

To set up a steamer:

Almost every tamale in Mexico is cooked by steaming. *Tamalerías* are large metal steamers made especially for cooking tamales. They look like tall stockpots. A shelf with holes for stacking tamales is placed on the bottom over an inch or two of boiling water. An opening under the shelf, on the outside of the pot, is for adding additional boiling water so the lid doesn't have to be removed during the cooking process. Some alternatives, if you have no *tamalería:* an Asian bamboo steamer; stainless steel vegetable steamer, opened flat, in a wide pot; or three water-filled tunafish cans or custard cups at the bottom of a wide pot with a nonfragile plate on top, with enough room for steam to escape along the sides. In any metal steamer, drop a few coins in the water— you know there's water in a metal steamer as long as you can hear the coins rattling.

To steam:

1. Pour water into the steamer. Be sure the water does not touch the rack. Lay any remaining husks on the rack to keep the tamales from sticking to it. If the tamale ends are open, arrange them vertically in the steamer so the *masa* doesn't fall out. Arrange other tamales horizontally and overlapping so steam can pass around each.

2. Cover the steamer tightly and bring to a boil. Reduce the heat to medium and steam for about 1 hour. Check the water level after 45 minutes, but do not remove the cover before then. Add boiling water if necessary.

3. Remove a tamale from the center of the steamer to see if it is done—the *masa* should pull away from the husk easily and be firm. Let the tamales rest for 10 minutes before serving. As with all tamales, peel away and discard the husks, then eat.

Sweet Tamales Made with Coarsely Ground Masa
Tamales Dulces

In Mexico, tamales are often sweet, a fact unknown to many people in the U.S. Husk-wrapped bundles of sweetened, coarse corn dough are eaten, as are most tamales, as early morning breakfasts or late light suppers. Think of them as Mexican muffins wafting the aroma of corn, and wash them down with a cup of *Café de Olla* (page 186), steaming Mexican chocolate, or pre-Hispanic corn gruel, *atole*.

Yield: about 25 medium tamales

For the corn husks:

See page 72

For the filling:

Prepare a filling before beginning the dough. Suggestions include: ¾ cup raisins; chopped fresh or dried papaya or mango with ½ cup ground nuts mixed into the *masa;* preserves or jam filling (about 2 cups); puréed fresh fruit such as peaches, plums, cherries, bananas, or apricots with ¼ cup white sugar for each cup of fruit, mixed into the *masa,* replacing the water; rum-soaked pineapple chunks with shredded coconut; puréed strawberries in the *masa* (replaces water) and served with puréed strawberries; and 1 cup toasted chopped nuts mixed with 1 cup *Cajeta* (page 164).

For the dough:

1⅓ cups butter or vegetable shortening

2 pounds (about 4 cups) coarsely ground *masa* from a tortillería (not *masa preparada,* because it has

1. Whip the butter or vegetable shortening with an electric mixer (or by hand) until the texture is fluffy and aerated, 5 minutes with a mixer, three times as long by hand with fast folding motions.

2. Add the *masa,* a handful at a time, with the baking powder, *piloncillo,* and salt. Mix well and continue to mix. If the mixture becomes too thick, add tepid water. This step

fat incorporated), or *masa* **made from 4 cups coarse** *masa harina* **reconstituted with 4 cups warm water (a general rule of thumb is that 2 pounds** *masa* **makes 25 medium-sized tamales)**

1 Tablespoon baking powder

1½ cups *piloncillo (panela)* **or dark brown sugar**

2 teaspoons kosher salt

takes about 10 minutes; you will feel the *masa* become light and fluffy with a spongy texture. The prepared *masa* is now ready to be spread onto husks and topped with a filling.

To assemble: (see page 74)

To steam: (see page 75)

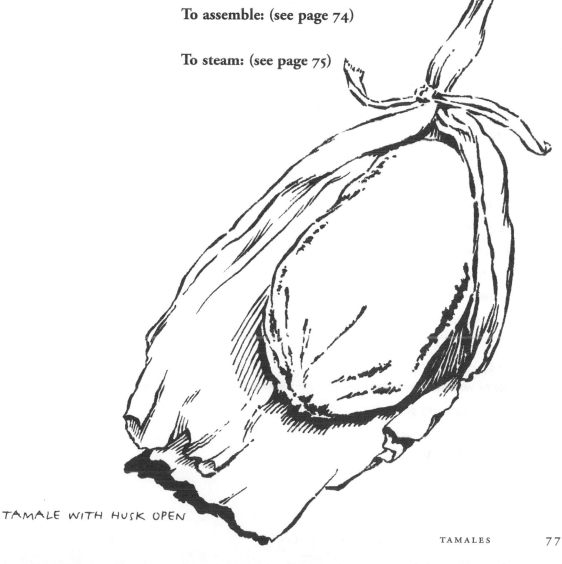

TAMALE WITH HUSK OPEN

Tamales Made with Coarsely Ground Masa and Vegetable Oil

Tamales de Aceite

Reyna entertains locals and tourists alike in her San Miguel de Allende, Guanajuato, home at her Friday noon cooking classes (page 213). The classes always end in a feast. One Friday she demonstrated how she makes tamales with healthful corn oil rather than butter or vegetable shortening. The texture is only slightly denser than the same tamales made with hydrogenated fat. Reyna likes chard, spinach, watercress, collard, and other leafy greens as stuffings. You can use these or choose a stuffing recipe given in this chapter.

To serve: Reyna places a tamale on its opened flat husk, surrounds it with Basic Cooked Tomato Sauce (page 32), and sprinkles it with toasted *pepítas* (shelled pumpkin seeds).

Yield: about 25 tamales

For the corn husks:
See page 72

For the dough:
2 pounds (about 4 cups) coarsely ground *masa* from a tortillería (not *masa preparada* because it has fat incorporated), or *masa* made from 4 cups coarse *masa harina* reconstituted with 4 cups Vegetable Broth (page 90) or warm water
¾ cup corn or vegetable oil
1 Tablespoon baking powder
1 Tablespoon kosher salt

1. Put the *masa* in a large bowl and work in the oil, ¼ cup at a time, with a heavy duty electric mixer for 5 minutes, three times as long by hand with fast folding motions.

2. Add the baking powder, salt, and oregano. Continue to mix, adding the broth a little at a time. This step takes about 10 minutes; you will feel the *masa* become light. This *masa* is not as fluffy as *masa* made with shortening or butter. The dough is now ready to be spread onto husks and topped with the filling.

2 Tablespoons dried Mexican
  oregano
1 cup Vegetable Broth (page
  90) or water

For the filling and assembly:
1 Tablespoon vegetable oil
2 onions, chopped
4 garlic cloves, chopped
4 jalapeño or serrano chiles,
  stemmed and chopped
  (seeds intact)
2 pounds chard or other leafy
  greens, washed, dried, and
  chopped
1 pound shredded quesillo de
  Oaxaca, mozzarella, or
  Monterey Jack cheese (low-
  fat cheeses work well as
  long as they melt)
1 cup chopped cilantro
Optional garnishes: Basic
  Cooked Tomato Sauce (page
  32), and 2 cups toasted
  pepitas (pumpkin seeds)

1. Heat the oil in a skillet and add the onions. Stir until golden and add the garlic and chiles. Continue to cook for another minute until light brown. Add the chard, turn off the heat, and cover the skillet for a few minutes to wilt the chard.

2. Place ¼ cup dough on the leaf. Spread it out, on the wide end, from side to side and about halfway up the leaf, using a spatula. Place a tablespoonful of filling on the dough, then a tablespoon of cheese. Sprinkle with cilantro. Fold over the sides and then flap the pointed end of the leaf over.

3. Continue with the remaining tamales and place the finished tamales in a bowl, open ends up, until ready to steam. Carefully arrange the tamales vertically (so the *masa* doesn't fall out when steaming) on a rack in a steamer lined with leftover husks.

To steam: (see page 75)

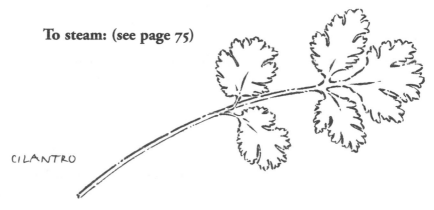

CILANTRO

Fresh Corn Tamales Wrapped in Fresh Corn Leaves

Uchepos

Sweet, fresh corn (rather than *masa*) makes these tamales some of the most popular in Mexico. And, they're easy to make. *Uchepos* are also called green corn tamales. They are not stuffed; their delicate sweetness and moist texture are delightful on their own. Green leaves from freshly shucked corn ears are used as wrappings, rather than dried husks. If you purchased corn that had its leaves removed, go ahead and use soaked husks. Esperancita (a nickname for Esperanza) says, "The trick to excellent green corn tamales is not to waste time—get the *uchepos* into a steamer, pronto, before the corn loses its natural sugar and becomes starchy." Pizzazz is traditionally supplied by Basic Cooked Tomatillo Sauce (page 34). A dollop of *Crema* (page 49) turns *uchepos* into a Breakfast of Champions.
Yield: about 36 tamales

For the corn leaves:

24 ears of corn on the cob, all outer leaves attached and undisturbed (no cuts or tears)

1. Cut around and through the leaves near the base of each corn ear (at the widest point), but not into the cob, using a heavy, sharp knife.
2. Carefully remove the largest whole leaves from the corn ears. Save the smaller leaves to line the steamer. Rinse well. Remove all the corn silk from the ears.

For the filling:

1 Tablespoon kosher salt

1. Starting at the small end and cutting toward the large end, cut the kernels off an ear of corn into a very large bowl. With the blunt side of the knife, scrape the sweet corn essence from the cob, starting at the large end and scraping toward the small end. Continue with the remaining corn.
2. In batches, grind the corn in a food processor or meat grinder (do not purée). Add the salt and mix thoroughly. Taste. The mixture should taste both sweet and slightly salty. The salty taste disappears when cooked. (Mexican corn is starchier than our own—add ¼ to ½ cup *masa* as a

thickener if the mixture is too wet to use as a filling.)

To assemble *uchepos:*

Put about ⅓ cup of the stuffing on the inside (curved inward) of a leaf, at the wide end. Fold the 2 sides over the stuffing, overlapping, like a business letter. Bring the narrow end over and flap. Tie with a husk ribbon (page 74) if desired. Gently place the finished tamale in a tamale steamer with the open end facing up so the filling does not fall out. Continue with the remaining leaves and filling.

Note: When corn is out of season and not too sweet, add granulated sugar by the tablespoon to taste, to the corn and salt mixture.

To steam: (See page 75)

Steam for 45 minutes. Check for doneness: the leaf should separate easily from the corn. If not, continue to steam 10 minutes. For an ancient steamer, Esperancita says to arrange about 8 corn cobs on the bottom of a large stock pot, overlapping. Pour in about 1 inch of water without covering the cobs. Cover with remaining leaves then arrange *uchepos* on top. *Uchepos* may be cooled, refrigerated, and reheated.

Variation:
Sweet Corn Tamales

Rather than seasoning with salt, use ½ cup *piloncillo (panela)* or dark brown sugar. In Esperancita's town of Pátzcuaro, Michoacán, some cooks add 2 teaspoons pulverized *canela* (pure Ceylon cinnamon) to greater differentiate these tamales from their nonsweet cousins.

Tamales Made with Finely Ground Masa Wrapped in Banana Leaves
Tamales con Hojas des Plátanos

Tamales made with finely textured *masa* and wrapped in banana leaves are southern-style and preferred in Oaxaca, Tabasco, Chiapas, and the Yucatán peninsula. The corn dough is so finely textured that when the tamales are steamed, the texture of the dough becomes similar to that of thick pasta. Exotic, charred beauties found in Mérida's market are baked in underground pits to intensify the banana leaf's heavenly perfume.
Yield: about 50 tamales

For the banana leaves:

12 banana leaves (defrosted if frozen)

1. Unfold and rinse the leaves, wiping off any powdery residue. Cut out the center vein by cutting with the grain from the pointed end (cutting from the wide end can tear the leaf) and you'll have two sides. With scissors, cut each side into rectangles about 8 by 10 inches. There will be wastage and many leaves will tear. When this happens, cut a smaller piece and put it over the tear, as a patch, when you add the *masa*.

2. Put the leaves in a steamer and steam until they become pliable. You can also run the pieces over a gas flame or electric burner so they have enough flexibility to fold. The leaf's color and texture change after 5 seconds on each side. Wrap in kitchen towels to keep the leaves moist.

For the dough:

4 pounds (about 8 cups) finely ground *masa* from a tortillería (not *masa preparada* because it has fat incorporated), or *masa* made from

1. Place the vegetable shortening in a bowl and beat it with a heavy duty electric mixer (or by hand) until fluffy, about 5 minutes.

2. Slowly add the *masa,* a handful at a time, beating it in with the *recado* and salt. After another 10 minutes the *masa* should be light and fluffy and it should be an even, light

8 cups *masa harina* and about 5⅓ cups warm water

2 Tablespoons red *recado*, or *achiote* paste

2 Tablespoons kosher salt

1 pound vegetable shortening

orange color with no splotches. If it's too thick, add up to 1 cup tepid water.

Filling suggestions: Fillings can be a squirt of salsa or an elaborate stewed mixture. Whatever you choose be sure it is highly flavored (hellfire-spicy is never an essential tamale trait). A few southern Mexican recommendations: black bean paste with *epazote* and vinegar-soaked red onion rings; *Oaxacan Mole Coloradito* (page 45) with cooked yam; Veracruzana cooked and mashed ripe plantains with chipotle chiles; or Campeche's sautéed plantain slices with *achiote* paste, sour orange juice, and a speck of habanero chile, steamed then grilled to char the leaf.

This is only the beginning. Other large, herby leaves such as *hoja santa* (anise-flavored) and fig are popular wrappers. Sometimes there is no filling; other times no *masa* at all: eggplant brushed with puréed *Chiles Chipotles en Adobo* (page 44) wrapped and grilled in fresh banana leaves is heaven sent; sliced waxy potatoes with *mole* are delectable steamed bundles; fresh fruit packaged in fresh fig leaves and grilled are divine.

To assemble:

1. Form slightly smaller-than-golfball-sized balls from the dough and arrange them on a tray. Cover with plastic wrap so they don't dry out.

2. Flatten a ball on the center of the smoothest side of a piece of banana leaf. Press it out, with your hands, to a 5-inch circle (no need for a ruler here—eyeball the size). *(Continued)*

3. Top with ⅓ cup filling (see suggestions), spreading it over the dough, keeping ½ inch away from the *masa* edge.

4. With two hands on the banana leaf, pick up one side and flap one third of the dough over. Lay the banana leaf back down (the dough will still be flapped). With two hands pick up the opposite side of the banana leaf and flap it over the other flapped part, keeping the banana leaf in place (don't lay it back down). Pick up the first section of leaf and flap it on top. Tuck the two sides under. The finished size is about 5 x 3 inches. If you'd like, tie long ribbons of steamed banana leaf around the packages for a decorative touch.

To steam:

1. Set up a steamer (page 75). Pour water into the steamer, being sure the water does not touch the rack.

2. Lay a few remaining leaves on the steamer rack. Place tamales on the rack, overlapping diagonally so steam can pass around each. If there are more leaves, cover the tamales with them to trap the steam.

3. Cover the steamer tightly and bring to a boil. Lower the heat to medium and steam for about 1 hour. Check the water level after 45 minutes, but do not remove the cover before then. To test for doneness, choose a tamale from the center and unwrap. The *masa* should pull away easily from the leaf. Let the tamales rest for 10 minutes before serving. As with all tamales, peel away and discard the leaves, then eat.

Giant Tamale of Masa and Eggs Wrapped in Banana Leaves
Brazo de Indio

Common everywhere in Yucatán is *brazo de indio,* an 8 x 2 x 1-inch thick tamale stuffed with hard-boiled eggs. Unlike flat, individual banana leaf–wrapped tamales from the region, these burrito-shaped monsters are sliced to serve. In Mérida, the herb *chaya* is chopped and mixed into the *masa,* but you can substitute fresh spinach. Rosario says the cooked tamales may be kept, refrigerated, for up to a week before resteaming or heating in a microwave oven. As with almost all traditional Mexican tamales, they may be frozen.
Yield: 6 rolls, about 12 servings (recipe may be divided in half)

For the banana leaves:

2 banana leaves, cut into six
    8 x 10-inch pieces (see page
    82), defrosted if frozen

For the dough and eggs:

4 cups *masa harina* and 2 cups
    water kneaded into a
    dough, or 2 pounds (about 4
    cups) finely ground *masa*
    from a tortillería (not *masa*
    preparada because it has fat
    incorporated) with enough
    warm water to soften into
    a pliable dough

¼ cup vegetable oil

1 teaspoon kosher salt

2 cups finely chopped spinach

12 hard-boiled eggs

1. Place the *masa* in a large bowl.

2. Add the oil, salt, and spinach. Mix well (see For the dough, page 73).

To assemble:

1. Cut the dough into 6 pieces of equal size. Flatten one piece on a banana leaf to an 8-inch square, about ⅛ inch thick, pressing it out with your hands. Bring the dough almost to the top and sides and 2 inches from the leaf bottom. Arrange 2 hard-boiled eggs end-to-end horizontally on the dough.

2. Pick up the leaf at the end toward you and flip it (with the dough) over the eggs. Lay the leaf down keeping the dough over the eggs. Flip the top leaf and dough over the
(Continued)

bottom dough-covered eggs. Lay the leaf down. Roll the leaf around the dough into a cylinder.

3. Enclose the tamale in a large square of foil and wrap snugly. Continue with the remaining tamales.

To steam:

1. Set up a tamale steamer, one large enough to accommodate the 6 tamales

2. Lay leaves on the steamer rack. Place the tamales on the rack. Cover with any remaining leaves.

3. Cover the steamer tightly and bring to a boil. Reduce the heat to medium and steam for 1 hour. Check the water level after 45 minutes, but do not remove the cover before then. To test for doneness, unwrap a tamale. The *masa* should pull away easily from the leaf. Let the tamales rest for 15 minutes before serving.

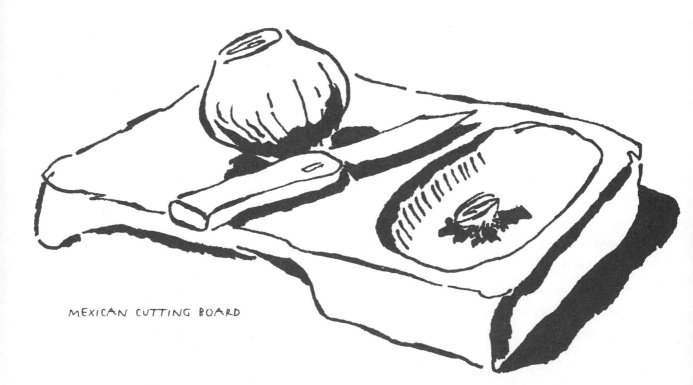

MEXICAN CUTTING BOARD

The tomato sauce:

1 Tablespoon vegetable oil

¼ cup chopped white onion

½ bell pepper, chopped

4 ripe tomatoes, chopped

1 whole habanero chile (or
   substitute jalapeño)

Salt

1. Heat the oil in a saucepan and add the onions. Cook, stirring, until transparent. Add the pepper and cook until the onion has lightly browned.

2. Add the tomatoes, whole chile, and salt to taste. Cook over medium heat for 10 minutes.

To serve:

⅓ cup toasted and ground
   pepítas (shelled pumpkin
   seeds), or ⅓ cup grated
   queso anejo or Parmesan
   cheese

1. Unwrap a tamale and discard the banana leaf. With a sharp knife, cut into thick 1½-inch slices and arrange on a serving plate.

2. Surround with tomato sauce. Rosario says to cut open the whole chile if your crowd likes spice, otherwise remove the chile. She also claims that older folks prefer the traditional flavor of toasted *pepítas* sprinkled over the tamales while young people go for Parmesan.

HABANERO CHILE

Soups

MEXICAN COOKS ARE FAMOUS FOR THEIR CAULDRONS OF bubbling vegetables, tomatoes, chiles, corn, beans, mushrooms, onions, garlic, herbs, and seasonings. Even on blistering hot days the traditional Mexican *comida corrida* (large midday meal) starts with a bowl of brothy vegetable soup. A tureen of soup and a basket of hot tortillas—what could be more soul satisfying on a chilly night? Tortilla soup is one of the most popular throughout the country; *pozole* is a full meal in a bowl; and *atole de grano* is an ancient Purépechan Indian corn and wild fennel soup—all are included here, among others, as representatives of Mexico's finest.

Basic Vegetable Broth
Sopa de Verdugas

Many Mexicans make vegetable broth on a daily basis, especially if their family is large. Everybody loves homemade soup, and this easy, mild broth is the basis of most of the favorites. Add the herbs and seasonings, sit back, and let the vegetables do all their own work. The broth will be ready in a few hours.

Yield: 2 quarts

1 large onion

8 garlic cloves

4 plum tomatoes

4 carrots, peeled

3 celery ribs

3 chayote or large zucchini squash

1 jalapeño chile, slit open with seeds intact

1 small bunch flat-leaf parsley

1 bunch cilantro (about 20 stems)

6 sprigs Mexican oregano, or 2 Tablespoons dried

10 black peppercorns

1 Tablespoon kosher salt

1. Coarsely chop the vegetables and place in a large stockpot with the chile and herbs. Add the peppercorns and salt.

2. Add 12 cups water (or enough to cover the vegetables) and bring to a boil, skimming any foam that forms on top. Lower the heat and simmer for about 2 hours, uncovered.

3. Strain the broth into another pot and discard the vegetables. Taste for seasoning, adding more salt if necessary. You may cool and refrigerate the broth for up to a week, and it may be frozen.

Cascabel Chiles in Broth
Sopa de Chile Cascabel

Cascabel chiles are dried, deep cordovan-colored, round chiles especially popular in Michoacán. They are called *cascabel,* or bell, because the 1-inch-diameter chiles rattle when shaken by their stems. When added to broth, the chiles float but don't make the broth spicy. They merely lend their fabulous, nutty, woodsy flavor. Roberto, who lives in Morelia, prepares this soup at his family's fonda where chile lovers spice up the broth by breaking open the thick-fleshed cascabels and letting the liquid and seeds run out.

Yield: 4 2-cup serving

2 quarts Vegetable Broth
(page 90)

4 cascabel chiles

2 Tablespoons fresh cilantro or
flat-leaf parsley, chopped,
for garnish

1. Heat the broth and add the chiles, whole, with stems attached.

2. Simmer for 20 minutes to soften the chiles. To serve, place 1 intact chile in each bowl of broth. Sprinkle with fresh herbs.

CASCABEL CHILES

Broth with Toasted, Thin Noodles
Sopa de Fideos

Mexican cooks have known for generations that broth tastes better when toasted noodles rather than raw noodles are cooked in the liquid. This is the same method as when you sauté rice to get that nutty flavor before adding liquid for rice pilaf. María-Luisa makes *sopa de fideos* almost every day at a *fonda* hidden within Taxco's mountainside market maze. She couldn't tell me why, but it's traditional to serve the noodle soup with *bolillos*, chewy French rolls, rather than tortillas, which are more typical soup accompaniments in the state of Guerrero.

Yield: 6 servings

3 Tablespoons vegetable oil

4 pasta nests (fideos), or
   Italian fidelini

1 cup chopped onion

6 garlic cloves, chopped

2 serrano chiles, chopped

2 tomatoes, chopped

¼ cup chopped cilantro

1 teaspoon kosher salt

8 grinds of black pepper

¼ cup grated queso añejo or
   Parmesan cheese

2 quarts Vegetable Broth
   (page 90)

1. Heat the oil in a large pot. Brown whole, unbroken pasta nests in the oil until golden, then remove with a slotted spoon and drain on paper towels.

2. Add the onions to the remaining oil and cook until golden. Add the garlic and chiles. Cook for another few minutes, stirring. Add the tomatoes, cilantro, salt, and pepper and cook together for 10 minutes.

3. Add the broth to the simmering mixture and bring to a boil. Break the pasta nests as you add them to the broth. Stir for a few minutes until the pasta is cooked. Ladle into bowls and sprinkle with cheese.

Tortilla Soup
Sopa de Tortilla

What makes tortilla soup so special are the thin strips of freshly fried tortillas piled on top of hot broth. Tortilla Soup, a textural masterpiece, changes its consistency depending on how fast you slurp your soup: At first the warm tortilla strips are crisp, but as they begin to absorb liquid, they take on a chewy texture. Finally, if you're doing more talking than eating, the tortillas dissolve into the liquid and thicken the broth. Added textural interest is supplied by buttery cubes of diced avocado. Pieces of soft cheese melt and become stringy, and a dollop of smooth, cool *Crema* (page 49) gilds the lily.

Yield: 6 servings

2 quarts Vegetable Broth (page 90)

2 *epazote* sprigs (optional)

2 guajillo or ancho chiles

8 stale tortillas

2 cups vegetable oil

1 cup ½-inch cubes quesillo de Oaxaca, mozzarella, or Monterey Jack cheese

1 avocado, cut into ½-inch cubes

1 cup Crema (page 49), crème fraîche, or sour cream

¼ cup chopped cilantro

2 limes, quartered

1. Bring the broth to a low simmer with the optional *epazote*. Taste for seasoning and, if necessary, add salt and pepper.

2. Remove the chile stems, seeds, and veins. Cut the chiles into 1-inch strips about a ¼ inch wide.

3. Stack the tortillas and cut in half with a large knife. Cut each pile into ¼-inch strips.

4. Heat the oil to hot and fry the chile strips just until they change color and darken. Remove from the oil with a slotted spoon and drain on absorbent paper towels. Fry the tortilla strips, a handful at a time, until they are golden. Drain on paper towels.

5. Ladle broth into bowls. Add a few chile strips, some cheese cubes, avocado cubes, and *crema*. Sprinkle with cilantro. Top with a pile of tortilla strips. Pass lime wedges with any remaining garnishes, because fresh lime juice makes the soup come to life.

Hominy and Grilled Vegetable Soup with Dried Chiles

Pozole

Pozole is my favorite solution for a cold winter's day meal—it's a monster bowl of knock-your-socks-off soup. The state of Jalisco offers three styles: white, green (with cilantro and green vegetables—mostly tomatillos), and red (terracotta-colored from dried chiles). Red is the most delectable with grilled vegetables. The earthy flavors of ancho, guajillo, and de árbol chiles qualify this soup for the big leagues.

Cooking traditional *pozole* can be time consuming and labor intensive. It requires cooking then soaking dried hominy in slaked lime, rubbing the loose skins off under running water, and finally removing the tiny germ from the base of each and every kernel so it opens like popcorn when cooked in broth. The wisest alternative is to purchase canned hominy found in some supermarkets and all Latino markets. With the flavor of grilled vegetables and chile, this soup matches the taste of Mexico's rich, meat-based *pozoles*.

Yield: 8 servings

2 ancho chiles

2 guajillo chiles

2 de árbol chiles

3 Tablespoons vegetable oil

1 large white onion, chopped

6 garlic cloves, chopped

1 recipe Vegetable Broth
   (page 90)

3 cans (29½ ounces each)
   Mexican-style hominy,
   drained and rinsed
   (Juanita's brand is good)

2 Tablespoons dried Mexican
   oregano

8 carrots, peeled

1. Soak the chiles in a quart of hot water for 30 minutes. Stem, seed, and put them in a blender container and purée with a ¼ cup water.

2. Heat 1 tablespoon of the oil in a large pot. Add the chopped onion and sauté until transparent. Add the garlic and chopped chiles and cook together for 5 minutes. Add the broth, hominy, and oregano. Bring to a boil, then reduce the heat and simmer for 30 minutes.

3. In another saucepan, boil the carrots whole until just cooked, about 20 minutes. Drain and dry.

4. Heat a grill or broiler. Grill the halved onions, zucchini, and carrots, brushing them with the remaining 2 tablespoons of oil to keep from sticking. When cooked and very browned (a little charred for flavor), cut into 2-inch chunks. Add to the hominy mixture with the salt and pepper. Simmer for

2 white onions, halved

4 zucchini, halved lengthwise

2 teaspoons kosher salt

8 grinds of black pepper

5 minutes and taste for seasoning. Add salt and pepper if necessary. Ladle into bowls and serve with garnishes for individual sprinkling at the table.

Note: *Pozole* is always accompanied by separate bowls of garnishes to pile on top of the soup: ½ head shredded green cabbage or iceberg lettuce; 1 chopped red onion; 12 sliced radishes; 4 limes cut into wedges; tortilla chips; a small dish of powdered chile; plus a bottle or two of commercial hot sauce.

DE ARBOL CHILE

Fresh Corn and Wild Fennel Top Soup
Atole de Grano

María sets up shop every evening at her spot on Plaza Gertrudis Bocanegra (a.k.a. the Plaza Chica) in Pátzcuaro, Michoacán, next to the Gran Hotel, on the corner. She sits on a low stool behind a narrow table with a four-person bench in front. Next to her on a wood-burning brazier is a large clay pot with her one product—*atole de grano*. People constantly stop by for a bowl or plastic cup "to go" of this specialty of the mountainous region west of Morelia.

María told me that she makes her tantalizing, steaming hot, green-colored soup with water, fresh corn, wild fennel tops, and salt. The counter holds small bowls of lime wedges and powdered chile. María's soup is highly flavored with anise. If fennel tops from your neighborhood market's Italian-style bulb fennel lack punch, cheat, and add anise flavoring, crushed seeds, or a little Pernod. The soup must have fennel flavor. (María revealed that she keeps bits of the fennel tops in her soup so that people know her *atole de grano* is the real thing and made with the wild herb, not flavorings and seeds). Also, Mexico's starchy field corn is a natural thickener for the liquid. To make it in the U.S. we have to add a little cornstarch to duplicate her soup's texture.

Yield: 6 servings

3 cups tightly packed wild fennel tops (feathery part only), or the bulbs and tops of Italian fennel bulbs plus flavoring

1 teaspoon cornstarch

6 ears of fresh corn

2 teaspoons kosher salt

3 limes, cut into wedges

2 Tablespoons chile powder

1. Add the fennel tops (or chopped bulbs and tops of Italian fennel) to 2 quarts of water in a large pot. Cover and bring to a boil. Boil for 20 minutes to extract all the flavor from the fennel. Turn off the heat and let the fennel steep for at least 1 hour. Remove the cooked fennel from the water and put it into a fine sieve over the pot of fennel water. Press down on the fennel, extracting all the juices. Discard the fennel.

2. Mix the cornstarch with a few tablespoons of the hot liquid. Stir to form a paste, then add more liquid and stir until blended. Pour into the fennel water.

3. Taste the broth carefully. If the fennel flavor is not assertive, add some anise flavoring at this point.

4. Reheat the liquid. Shuck the corn ears and remove all the silk. Cut 3 of the ears into 4 pieces each and put them in the boiling water. Scrape the kernels off the other 3 ears and add to the water. Add the salt and boil until the corn is cooked—María's is very well cooked. Remove any scum that forms on the surface.

5. To serve, add a few pieces of corn plus corn kernels and liquid to each bowl. Serve with lime wedges and a tiny dish of chile powder.

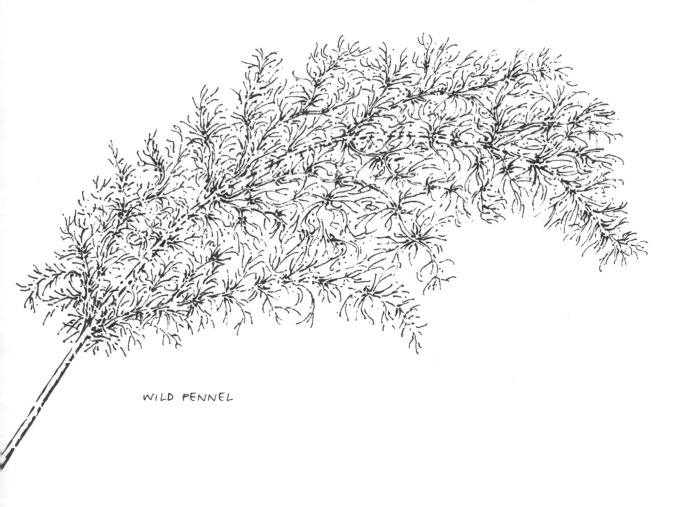

WILD FENNEL

SUSANA TRILLING'S

Oaxacan Corn Soup
Esquites

Every evening at about 5 P.M., vendors pedal their bicycle-food carts to designated spots on city streets in Central and Southern Mexico with steaming vats of the field-corn soup known as *esquites*. Vendors embellish the *epazote*-flavored liquid with chile powder and lime or grated cheese after ladling it into plastic cups "to go." Compare *esquites* with *Atole de Grano* (page 96) for an interesting Mexican regional difference. *Esquites* is one of many Mexican everyday dishes that Susana teaches at her Oaxacan cooking school (page 213). *Yield: 12 servings*

For the soup:

12 ears of corn

4 large, fresh *epazote* sprigs, or 2 rounded Tablespoons dried

2 Tablespoons butter

1 white onion, finely chopped

6 garlic cloves, finely chopped

1 Tablespoon kosher salt

8 grinds of black pepper

1. Trim the kernels from the corncobs with a sharp, heavy knife. There should be about 8 cups.

2. Add the corncobs (not the kernels) to a large pot with 3 quarts of water (or more to cover). Add 2 of the *epazote* sprigs. Cover the pot and bring the liquid to a boil, then lower the heat and simmer for 30 minutes.

4. In a heavy stockpot, heat the butter and add the onion. Sauté the onion until it is transparent. Add the corn kernels and the garlic. Stir for about 20 minutes, until the onion and corn kernels start to brown.

5. Add the corncob broth through a strainer, retaining 3 cobs for flavor. Add the cobs and remaining *epazote* to the broth. Cover and bring to a boil, then lower the heat and simmer for 1 hour. Add salt and pepper, stir, then taste for seasoning.

For the garnish:

8 Tablespoons mayonnaise

3 limes, quartered

1 cup grated queso añejo or Parmesan cheese

1 Tablespoon chile powder

1. Ladle the soup into each of 12 bowls.

2. Add a 2-teaspoon dollop of mayonnaise to each bowl. Sprinkle with juice from a lime wedge and scatter with a spoonful of cheese. Top with a sprinkle of chile powder (guajillo or de árbol preferred) mixed with salt if desired.

Black Bean Soup
Sopa de Frijoles Negroes

Black bean soup is rarely served in Mexico because black beans (the bean of choice in southern Mexico) are offered at almost every meal and they're served on the soupy side, in a side bowl. (This soup could easily be served as a side of knock-your-socks-off flavored beans in Oaxaca). Black bean soup, a Cuban influence, is enjoyed on the Yucatán peninsula, especially in the state of Quintana Roo—home to Cancún and Cozumel and a bean's toss off Castro's island. The soup must retain its black color. This happens only when the beans are slow-simmered for a very long time. Soaking and precooking only drains away color and you end up with gray beans. Mexicans never soak beans before cooking, anyway.

Yield: 8 servings

1 pound black beans

1 white onion, peeled and halved

4 *epazote* sprigs, or 2 rounded Tablespoons dried, or 1 small bunch of cilantro, tied

2 Tablespoons vegetable oil

2 jalapeño or serrano chiles, stemmed and chopped

1 large white onion, chopped

6 garlic cloves, chopped

1 Tablespoon cumin seed

1 tomato, chopped

1 Tablespoon kosher salt

8 grinds of black pepper

4 limes, quartered

1½ cups Crema (page 49), crème fraîche, or sour cream (low fat is fine)

1. Pick through the beans for pebbles, then rinse.

2. Put the beans in a pot with 10 cups of water. Add the halved onion and *epazote* or cilantro and bring to a boil. Lower the heat and simmer, covered, for 1 hour.

3. Heat the oil in a skillet and sauté the chiles with the chopped onion, garlic, and cumin seed until golden brown. Add the tomato and continue to cook for 3 minutes.

4. Remove the onion and herbs from the beans and discard. Add the sautéed onion mixture to the beans. If you especially like the flavor of *epazote* or cilantro, add additional chopped leaves or 1 tablespoon of dried and bring the beans to a boil, then simmer, uncovered, for 10 minutes. Add salt and pepper. Squeeze the juice of 1 lime into the soup and taste for seasoning. To serve, spoon a dollop of *crema* atop each bowl of soup. Serve with plenty of lime wedges.

Variation: Black bean soup may be served as a purée. Cool the soup to warm, then, in batches, pour it into a blender or processor and purée. If you'd like, blend the *crema* with the beans. Reheat to a simmer.

MERCEDES ARTEAGA TOVAR'S

Lentil Soup with Plantains
Sopa de Lentejas

Mercedes (page 212) says this old lentil soup recipe has been in her family for genera-tions. Catholics all over Mexico serve lentil soup with plantains during Lent. It's also a popular dish to serve during Day of the Dead celebrations. Protein-rich lentils are a splendid change from beans, especially when they're cooked in soup that's perfectly spiced, then blessed with sweet plantain flavor.

Yield: 8 servings

4 Tablespoons vegetable oil

1 large white onion, finely chopped

3 garlic cloves, finely chopped

½ teaspoon cumin seed

3 grinds of fresh allspice, or ¼ scant teaspoon ground

2 tomatoes, finely chopped

2 teaspoons kosher salt

8 grinds of black pepper

1 cup chopped cilantro

1½ cups brown lentils

2 quarts Vegetable Broth (page 90)

2 ripe plantains (black skins), peeled and sliced on the diagonal

2 limes, quartered

1. Heat 2 tablespoons of the oil in a large pot. Sauté the chopped onion until transparent, then add the garlic, cumin, and allspice and cook until the mixture is golden brown. Add the tomatoes, salt, pepper, and half the cilantro. Cook together for 3 minutes.

2. Add the lentils and broth. Bring to a boil, cover, reduce the heat, and simmer for 1 hour. Taste for seasoning.

3. Meanwhile, heat the remaining 2 tablespoons of oil in a skillet and brown the plantain slices on both sides.

4. Ladle the soup into bowls and top each with plantain slices. Sprinkle with the remaining cilantro. Serve with fresh lime wedges.

Variation: Mercedes easily turns this into a creamy lentil soup without using any cream. Her hint: Don't brown the plantains for cream soup; slowly cook them until they're soft and pale golden. Slightly cool the completed soup (with the plantains but without the cilantro garnish) and purée. Reheat and garnish with the cilantro and lime.

ROBERTA CARMEN MINUTO'S

Cream of Pumpkin Soup with Chipotle Chiles

Crema de Calabazas con Chiles Chipotles

Roberta says her soup "is better than my mother's because she was such a crummy cook—my great aunt taught me how to make this old recipe, one I remember from visiting her home as a kid." Roberta's aunt lived near Cordoba, Veracruz, and Roberta lives just outside Veracruz City where she works in the wholesale fruit business. As a single woman who eats out most of the time, cooking isn't on her priority list, but Roberta enjoys whipping up a batch of her favorite smoky, spicy soup on weekends. Of course you may substitute milk for cream, but be sure the milk never boils or it will curdle.

Yield: 8 to 10 servings

1 cooking pumpkin or orange-pulp winter squash (butternut is fine), 5 pounds

8 garlic cloves, unpeeled

3 *chiles chipotles en adobo* (2 if you want less spice)

1 cup heavy cream

6 cups water

1 Tablespoon kosher salt

8 grinds of black pepper

1 teaspoon ground *canela,* or ½ teaspoon cinnamon

¼ cup *piloncillo (panela)* or dark brown sugar

3 Tablespoons chopped cilantro

6 cilantro sprigs, for garnish

1 cup Crema (page 49) or crème fraîche (optional)

1. Preheat the oven to 400°F.

2. Halve the squash, scoop out the seeds, and place the cut sides down in a roasting pan. Add ¼ inch hot water to the pan and bake until the squash is soft, about 1 hour. Set the squash aside to cool slightly.

3. Toast (page 28) the garlic cloves, cool them enough to handle, and slip off the skins.

4. Blend the garlic with the chipotles and a spoonful of squash. Add a few cups squash flesh to the blender and purée until smooth. Put the mixture in a large pot. Purée the remaining squash, adding water if necessary, and add to the pot.

5. Add the cream to the puréed squash-chile mixture. Add the water, salt, pepper, *canela, piloncillo,* and chopped cilantro. Bring the soup to a boil, then reduce the heat and simmer for 20 minutes. Taste and adjust the seasoning. Ladle into bowls and top with a sprig of cilantro and a drizzle of the optional *crema.*

Garlic Soup
Sopa de Ajo

Buy the largest head of garlic you can find for garlic soup because large cloves make the job of peeling and chopping easier—but don't use elephant garlic because its flavor is too delicate. While sautéeing and simmering, the garlic melts into a blissfully sweet, yet intensely flavored potion. After the soup is in bowls, scatter with croutons if you like. Mercedes (page 212) prefers to cut them small for a fancy dinner or large (baguette size) for a home-style meal. She swears by her easy garlic soup for curing both flu and miserable hangovers. If *sopa de ajo* can't scare off a cold, nothing can—there's enough garlic here to stop a werewolf in its tracks.

Yield: 4 servings

2 Tablespoons olive oil

1 large onion, chopped

1 garlic head (about 12 good-
   sized cloves), chopped

5 cups water

½ cup chopped flat-leaf
   parsley leaves

2 teaspoons kosher salt

8 grinds of black pepper

1 egg, lightly whisked
   (optional)

1 cup toasted croutons
   (optional)

1. Heat the oil in a pot and add the onion. Cook until the onion is transparent. Add the garlic and continue to cook until the mixture is caramelized.

2. Put the onion and garlic in a blender container with ½ cup of the water. Purée and pour the liquid back into the pot. Add the remaining water to the blender and blend for a few seconds (to get all the juices left in the container), then add the liquid to the pot. Add the parsley, salt, and pepper. Bring to a boil.

3. Stir the optional egg into the boiling liquid. The texture resembles Chinese egg drop soup. Taste for seasoning and top with optional croutons.

GARLIC CLOVES

Corn Chowder with Golden Chiles
Crema de Elote

I tried this soup at Eva's home in Mérida. It seemed a bit odd because she served this after our discussion about regional foods and how so few cream soups are eaten in Yucatán. It turns out that she was brought up on creamy corn chowder because in the sixties her mother visited Puebla, where she was given the recipe by an elderly aunt who was originally from Guerrero. Over the years the regional yellow chile has changed in the recipe, but no matter—this soup is packed with complex flavors thanks to toasted chiles and sweet, freshly scraped corn. The soup looks all dressed up with an optional swirl of brick-red salsa made with mild dried ancho chiles.

Yield: 6 servings

3 mild banana chiles, or 1 spicy perón chile (a.k.a. manzano), or ½ extremely hot habanero, toasted (page 28), stemmed, and seeded

4 ears of sweet corn, or 3 cups frozen kernels if you're desperate for corn soup in the winter months

4 cups milk, whole or low fat

2 Tablespoons vegetable oil

1 large white onion, chopped

6 garlic cloves, chopped

2 teaspoons cumin seed

2 teaspoons kosher salt

8 grinds of black pepper

1 Tablespoon sugar (optional)

3 Tablespoons chopped flat-leaf parsley

1. Put the toasted chiles in a blender or processor and purée, adding a few tablespoons water if necessary.

2. Husk and remove the silk from the ears of corn. With a large, sharp knife, scrape the kernels off the cobs into a large bowl. With the blunt end of the knife, scrape the remaining kernels and milky juices from the cobs into the bowl. Spoon the corn into a blender and blend, scraping down the sides of the blender, pulsing the machine, adding about ½ cup of the milk. Be sure to keep some corn texture.

3. Heat 1 tablespoon of the oil in a large pot and add the onion. Sauté until it is transparent. Add the garlic and cumin seed and cook until golden, but do not brown. Add the onion mixture to the corn-chile purée. Blend again.

4. In the same pot, heat the remaining tablespoon of oil and pour in the corn mixture. Add the remaining milk. Do not boil or the milk will curdle.

5. Add the salt and pepper. Simmer for 15 minutes. Taste for seasoning. You may want to add up to 1 tablespoon sugar if you used frozen corn. Sprinkle with parsley and serve.

Salads and Pickled Vegetables

ALTHOUGH SALADS AREN'T MUCH OF A MEXICAN TRADITION, they're part of everyone's healthy eating today. Salads run the gamut from the more-popular-than-ever Caesar, with crunchy romaine coated with creamy anchovy dressing and topped with garlic-spiked croutons; or a simple pile of shredded cabbage with guacamole, *crema,* and radish slices; to a spoonful of vinegary pickled vegetables that adds just the right zing to any rich melted cheese dish.

Pickled Vegetables
Verduras en Escabeche (en Vinagre)

Bowls of preserved, pickled, vinegared vegetables are standard fare on market *fonda* counters, in homes, and in fine restaurants. This recipe is from a coastal village in the west coast state of Sinaloa, where it was faultless atop Francisca's refried bean *sopes*. *Escabeche* is served as a condiment and is a perfect foil for Mexico's rich sauces and cheesy dishes (even if they are low in fat these days). Almost any vegetable can be pickled in vinegar; carrots, cauliflower, green beans, cactus paddles, chiles, bell peppers, garlic cloves, thick onion slices, pearl onions, and baby potatoes are especially successful. Mixtures of any of the above are popular. Prepare this one at least a day ahead of serving, to allow the flavors to blend. Serve at room temperature.

Yield: about 4 cups

3 Tablespoons vegetable oil

12 garlic cloves

1 cup sliced carrots

1 cup small cauliflower
   sections

8 jalapeño chiles, slit vertically
   down one side

1 large onion, sliced vertically

1 cup mild vinegar: cider,
   white wine, or herb-flavored

1 cup water

2 bay leaves

2 cloves

3 Tablespoons dried Mexican
   oregano

6 peppercorns

2 teaspoons kosher salt

1. Heat the oil and add the garlic cloves. Sauté until the garlic turns golden and remove from the oil. Add the carrots to the hot oil and cook for 2 minutes, then add the cauliflower, chiles, and onion. Continue to cook and stir for another 2 minutes. The vegetables must remain crisp.

2. Add the cooked garlic, vinegar, water, bay leaves, cloves, oregano, peppercorns, and salt. Bring to a boil, then remove from the heat.

3. Transfer the vegetables and liquid to a large, clean, hot jar. Let cool, then cover with a tight-fitting lid. Let the *escabeche* develop flavors overnight in the refrigerator. The refrigerated oil will become cloudy—let the pickled vegetables sit at room temperature for 10 minutes before serving and the cloudiness will disappear.

Pickled Chipotle Chiles
Chipotles en Vinagre

Señora Socorro Brun de López's old Puebla recipe is perfectly suited to various rich cheese dishes beloved by Poblanos. Smoky, spicy, vinegary chiles add just the right touch of regional flavor boosters to creamy entrées; they add wonderful and complex flavor layers to vegetable stews and soups; or use the flavored vinegar mixed with good olive oil to dress your salad greens.

Yield: about 4 cups

4 ounces (about 25) dried chipotle chiles, stemmed and seeded if desired

2 cups hot water

2 cups cider or white vinegar

1 cup *piloncillo (panela),* or dark brown sugar

2 carrots, peeled and sliced

2 cloves

1 bouquet garni

1 Tablespoon kosher salt

1 small white onion, sliced

1. Rinse the chiles carefully, then put them in a pot with 2 cups of boiling water. Add the vinegar, *piloncillo,* carrots, cloves, bouquet garni, and salt. Bring the liquid back to a boil, then turn down the heat and simmer, covered, for 30 minutes.

2. Uncover the pot and add the onion. Remove from the heat and cool. This can keep in the refrigerator for months.

ANGEL MENDOZA'S

Caesar Salad
Ensalada de Caesar

Most people agree that Caesar salad was created for gringos in 1924 in the nothern Baja city of Tijuana by an Italian immigrant, Caesar Cardini. Today it's the southern tip of the Baja peninsula that attracts Caesar lovers, at Pancho's restaurant (page 214). Wash down chef Angel Mendoza's anchovy-enhanced salad with one of John Bragg's obscure tequilas or mezcals—his accumulation is reported to be the largest drinkable collection in the world. *¡Salud!*

Yield: 6 servings

2 heads romaine lettuce, hearts and tender leaves only

1 *bolillo* or 6-inch French or Italian roll

3 Tablespoons butter

2 garlic cloves, minced

1. Clean the lettuce, dry, and tear into pieces. Crisp in the refrigerator.

2. Prepare the croutons by cutting the bread into 1-inch cubes. Heat the butter in a large skillet and add the bread cubes. Sauté the cubes over medium heat until they are lightly toasted. Add the garlic and cook until the garlic is golden. Or, for a fat-free alternative, toast the cubes in a single layer on a baking sheet in a 300°F oven for 15 to 20 minutes, eliminating the butter and garlic.

For the dressing:

3 anchovy fillets

2 garlic cloves

1 egg

6 grinds of black pepper

¼ teaspoon Dijon mustard

3 drops of Worcestershire sauce

3 drops of Maggi seasoning

2 Tablespoons white vinegar

6 Tablespoons fruity olive oil

1. Mash together the anchovy fillets and garlic with a fork in a medium-size bowl, or with a mortar and pestle.

2. Add the egg (use only the freshest—preferably from free-range chickens—refrigerated, perfectly clean, and from a reliable source, because it's used raw in the salad; if you have doubts, eliminate it) and the remaining ingredients and whisk together until creamy.

To assemble:

**Chilled lettuce, croutons, and
just-made dressing**

**⅓ cup grated queso añejo or
Parmesan cheese**

1. In a large bowl, toss the lettuce and croutons (including the browned garlic) with enough dressing to coat the leaves—do not drench in dressing.

2. Divide the salad among 6 salad plates. Sprinkle with freshly grated cheese and offer additional freshly ground black pepper.

HEADS OF GARLIC

Simply Sensational Green Salad
Ensalada Verde

Crisp romaine lettuce is a natural complement to Mexican food. As good as it is, pungent Caesar salad can get boring even though you still crave cold, crunchy romaine spears. This green salad offers an unforgettable dressing made by adding a splash of bottled chipotle chile hot sauce to a simple vinaigrette. Many brands can be found in shops and catalogs that specialize in bottled hell-raisers—they're listed in Mail-Order Sources (page 204). If you have some homemade *Chiles Chipotles en Adobo* (page 44), by all means use a teaspoon of the fantastic purée.

Yield: 1 cup

1 head romaine lettuce, washed, dried, and chilled

3 Tablespoons virgin olive oil

1 Tablespoon lime juice

1 teaspoon sugar

¼ teaspoon kosher salt

6 grinds of black pepper

1 teaspoon bottled spicy chile chipotle sauce (Búfalo brand is good)

1. Tear the lettuce leaves into 2-inch pieces and put them in a salad bowl.

2. In a small bowl, mix the oil, lime juice, sugar, salt, and pepper. Add the chipotle chile hot sauce, whisk thoroughly, and taste for seasonings. Toss with the lettuce.

Hearts of Palm and Papaya Salad
Ensalada de Palmitos y Papaya

Hearts of palm is a popular salad ingredient along Mexico's Pacific coast, where coconut groves blot out everything else for miles on end, and where Lupita lives with her family south of Puerto Vallarta. Tender hearts of palm are only available canned in the U.S., but still contribute to a sensational salad when papayas are in season. Lupita showed me how to dry Hawaiian papaya seeds to make cracked papaya seed dressing (the spicy flavor is somewhere between black pepper and nasturtium seeds) for this, her favorite salad.

Yield: 4 servings

1 ripe Hawaiian papaya

1 teaspoon sugar

2 Tablespoons plus 1 teaspoon fruity olive oil

1 Tablespoon fresh lime juice

¼ teaspoon kosher salt

1 can (8 ounces) hearts of palm, drained and rinsed

8 large lettuce leaves, washed and dried

1 slice mild red onion, broken into rings

1. Cut the papaya in half lengthwise. Scoop out the seeds, put them in a strainer, and rinse. Cover the papaya in plastic wrap and reserve. Arrange the seeds on a baking sheet and bake in a 350°F oven, turning twice, for 15 minutes. Do not overbake the seeds; if they become very dry they will be tasteless. Cool and dry.

2. Place enough seeds in a mortar and crush them with a pestle to a coarse grind (or use the bottom of a heavy skillet) so you have at least 1 tablespoon.

3. In a bowl, dissolve the sugar in the oil, lime juice, and salt. Add the hearts of palm and mix.

4. Arrange the lettuce on a serving plate. Slice the reserved papaya and place the slices attractively over the lettuce. Mound the hearts of palm and juices in the center of the plate. Cover with onion slices. Sprinkle with the crushed papaya seeds.

Jícama and Oranges with Fresh Chiles
Ensalada de Jícama y Naranja

Señora Anguiano instructed, "The sweetest jícamas always have their leaves attached," when she told me how to prepare this effortless salad at her vegetable booth in Guadalajara's huge Mercado Libertad. Jícama salads are the favorites of her teenage daughters, who are always watching their weight. This dressing tops their list because it contains no oil. Notice the similarity between Mexican salads and salsas. When this salad is finely chopped it makes a fine fresh salsa. In the Fall when pomegranates are in season, sprinkle the salad with red seeds.

Yield: 4 servings

3 red onion slices, ⅛ inch thick

1 jícama, 4 to 5 inches in diameter

3 navel oranges

3 chopped serrano chiles, or ½ teaspoon chile powder (or to taste depending upon variety)

2 Tablespoons finely chopped cilantro

½ teaspoon kosher salt

6 grinds of black pepper

1 pomegranate

1. Cut the onion slices into eighths, pie-style. Put into a bowl of cold water to soak and become mild.

2. Peel the jícama with a sharp knife. Cut the tuber in half and slice both halves into ⅛-inch slices. Julienne. Put into a bowl.

3. Peel the oranges and cut into sections, leaving behind the white membrane. (Do this step over the bowl with the jicama to catch the juices.) Mix in the chile, cilantro, salt, and freshly ground pepper.

4. Drain the onion and pat dry with paper towels. Add to the jicama mixture. Refrigerate for at least 1 hour. Stir well before serving and adjust the seasoning if necessary. Sprinkle with pomegranate seeds, if available.

POMEGRANATE

Chayote Salad
Ensalada de Chayote

Chayote squash is eaten all over Mexico—it's their equivalent of our summer zucchini or yellow crookneck. Chayote grows abundantly along the shores of Lake Chapala in Jalisco where you can see the trellises (similar to those used for grape vines) with workers tending the vines and harvesting from underneath. Chayote is usually seen as a pale green, pear-shaped squash, about 6 inches long and 3 inches wide. Another variety is dark green with short, spiky hair growing all over the surface. This squash must be peeled before using. Both varieties are interchangable. Chayote is extremely mild—almost bland—so it's a fine foil for spicy sauces. The texture is similar to that of cucumber, and this recipe may remind you of a refreshing cucumber salad. Years ago chayote was available for only a short period each year, and then only in Latino markets. Supermarkets stock it now, right next to the other squash.

Yield: 4 servings

2 chayote squash (smooth, light green skin)

4 Tablespoons olive oil

1 garlic clove, minced

1 jalapeño or serrano chile, stemmed, seeded, and minced

4 cilantro sprigs, chopped

1 lime, juiced

2 teaspoons sugar

6 grinds of black pepper

½ teaspoon kosher salt

1. Cut the chayote in half horizontally. Discard the pit. Turn the chayote over, cut side down, and slice it into lengthwise strips, as thin as possible. Stack 5 or 6 slices and cut into matchstick strips about ⅛ inch wide.

2. Bring 4 quarts of water to a boil and cook the chayote until just cooked, or even slightly underdone, about 1 minute. Put the chayote in a colander and run cold water over the squash to stop the cooking. Let the water drain for a few minutes, then pat the chayote dry with a towel and put the squash in a bowl.

3. In a small bowl, stir together the oil, garlic, chile, cilantro, lime juice, sugar, pepper, and salt. Pour the dressing over the chayote. Toss.

Lentil and Corn Salad
Ensalada de Lentejas y Elotes

Reyna's lentil salad is always a hit with her cooking students (see page 213). Simple, nutritious, and packed with flavor, the delightful presentation is achieved by placing a fresh corn leaf on a salad plate and spooning the salad mixture on top. Mexicans use a great deal of lentils because the cheap, protein-packed legumes are a change from their ever-present beans. If you prefer fresh chiles, Reyna says to add finely chopped fresh green and/or red jalapeños or serranos.

Yield: 8 servings

6 ears of fresh corn with
    leaves attached

1 cup sprouted lentils

1 teaspoon prepared mustard

1 teaspoon kosher salt

½ teaspoon sugar

¼ cup virgin olive oil

1 lime, juiced

1 cup finely chopped mild
    onion

Optional: Piquín chile powder
    to taste, or fresh chile

1. Carefully remove 8 of the largest, best-looking leaves from the corn ears. Wash, dry, and trim 1 inch off the wide bottom half. Trim off any brown tips and reserve the leaves for garnish, wrapped in plastic and refrigerated.

2. With a large heavy knife, scrape the corn kernels off the cobs directly into a large bowl. Bring 2 quarts of water to a boil and add the kernels. Cook for a few minutes, just until they are tender. Drain the kernels and run under cold water.

3. Bring another 2 quarts of water to a boil in the same pot and add the sprouted lentils. Boil the lentils for 1 minute, quickly drain, and run under cold water in the strainer with the corn. Put the corn and lentils in the large bowl and refrigerate.

4. Whisk together the mustard, salt, and sugar. Slowly add the oil, whisking. Add the lime juice and whisk again, blending the ingredients completely. When the corn and lentils are chilled, add the onion, pour the vinaigrette over, and combine.

5. Lay a corn leaf on each of 8 salad plates. Spoon some of the corn-lentil mixture on each leaf. Sprinkle with chile powder and serve.

Avocado, Tomato, and Fresh Cheese Salad
Ensalada de Aguacate, Jitomate y Panela

The first time I saw this simple to prepare salad in a Mexico City restaurant over 10 years ago I immediately thought of *caprese,* the classic Italian antipasto of alternating slices of mozzarella cheese and half-ripe tomatoes in olive oil and herbs. *Panela* cheese, red-ripe tomatoes, and avocado slices in olive oil and lime juice transform the combination to distinctly Mexican.

Yield: 4 servings

2 large ripe tomatoes

6 ounces queso fresco such as panela or ranchero cheese

2 ripe but not soft avocados, peeled and pitted

2 ⅛-inch slices of red onion

6 red radishes

5 Tablespoons extra virgin olive oil

2 Tablespoons fresh lime juice

½ teaspoon sugar

¼ teaspoon kosher salt

6 grinds of black pepper

2 Tablespoons coarsely chopped cilantro leaves

1. Slice the tomatoes, cheese, and avocados into ⅛ inch slices. Thinly slice the radishes.

2. On a serving plate, alternate the tomato, cheese, and avocado slices in rows or circles. Break the onion slices into rings and arrange on top. Sprinkle with the radish slices.

3. Combine the oil, lime juice, sugar, salt, and pepper and mix well. Drizzle over the salad and sprinkle with chopped cilantro leaves.

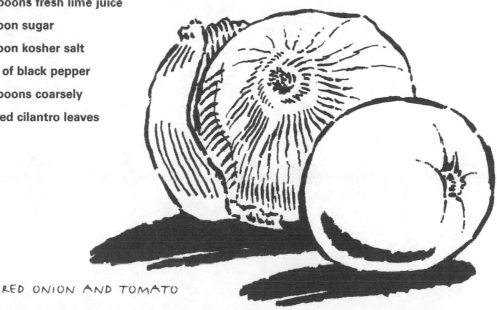

RED ONION AND TOMATO

Rice, Beans, Pastas, and Potatoes

FULL MEXICAN MEALS, ESPECIALLY THE MAIN AFTERNOON MEAL, *comida,* usually begin with a simple vegetable broth, followed by a small dish of rice or pasta, then a main course. Beans and tortillas are served alongside. This tried-and-true format can change if, for example, the main dish is a rice-and-vegetable casserole or a huge bowl of *caldo* (thick soup). In that case, maybe ice cream or custard is included in the *prix fixe* if *comida corrida* is eaten at a *fonda* or casual restaurant. Anyway, Mexican rice dishes are legendary; their pots of beans renowned; *sopa secas* (dry pasta dishes) addictive; and potatoes so sweet, they're perfect simply boiled.

Mexican Rice Pilaf
Arroz Mexicana

Except along the eastern shore of Mexico around Veracruz, Mexicans don't eat plain steamed rice very often. What you get in homes, *fondas,* and restaurants is flavorful rice pilaf made with sautéed onions and homemade broth. Mexicans rinse medium grain rice to remove surface starches so it's never gummy. Drain and shake this rice dry in the strainer before adding to the hot onions.

Yield: 4 servings

1 cup medium-grain white rice

1½ Tablespoons vegetable oil

¼ cup finely chopped onion

1 garlic clove, finely chopped

2 cups boiling Vegetable Broth (page 90) or water

1 jalapeño or serrano chile, slit down the side with seeds intact

¼ scant teaspoon kosher salt (adjust salt to the saltiness of your broth)

4 grinds of black pepper

1. Rinse the rice under running water until the starches run clear. Drain well, then shake the strainer to rid the rice of all moisture.

2. Heat the oil in a large saucepan (with cover) and sauté the onion until transparent. Add the garlic and cook until golden. Add the rice and stir, coating the grains with oil. Continue to stir until the rice is just beginning to cook and change color.

3. Add the hot broth to the rice. Add the chile, salt, and pepper. Bring to a boil, cover, turn down the heat, and simmer for 25 minutes. Turn off the heat and let the rice rest for 10 minutes before removing the cover. Fluff the grains with a fork. Remove the chile before serving.

Mexican Red Rice
Arroz Rojo

Mexican red rice is the ubiquitous rice served in homes and *fondas* with *comida,* either as a separate dish after a simple brothy soup, or before, or with, the main dish. Red rice has all the flavors of Mexico, and can be labeled as comfort food for the entire population. Many people add a few tablespoons each of fresh peas and diced carrots when adding the liquid.

Yield: 4 servings

1 cup medium-grain white rice

1½ Tablespoons vegetable oil

¼ cup finely chopped onion

1 garlic clove, finely chopped

2 tomatoes, blanched,
    skinned, cored, and puréed

¼ scant teaspoon kosher salt
    (adjust salt to the saltiness
    of the broth)

4 grinds of black pepper

1 jalapeño or serrano chile,
    slit down the side with
    seeds intact

2 cups boiling Vegetable Broth
    (page 90) or water

1. Rinse the rice under running water until the starches run clear. Drain well, then shake the strainer to rid the rice of all moisture.

2. Heat the oil in a large saucepan (with cover) and sauté the onion until transparent. Add the garlic and cook until golden. Add the rice and stir, coating the grains with oil. Continue to stir until the rice is just beginning to cook and change color.

3. Add the tomato purée to the sizzling rice. Add the salt and pepper. Add the whole chile and the hot broth, bring to a boil, cover, turn down the heat, and simmer for 25 minutes. Turn off the heat and let the rice rest for 10 minutes before removing the cover. Fluff the grains with a fork. Remove the chile before serving.

Yucatán Yellow Rice
Arroz Amarillo

The color of this rice is wonderful—especially with the addition of red and green pepper slices. Bijol coloring powder (Bijol can be purchased in Latino and Caribbean markets) adds the bright yellow that gives this rice the regional stamp of the Yucatán peninsula, but you can substitute turmeric or 1 tablespoon *achiote* paste for Bijol.
Yield: 4 servings

1 cup medium-grain white rice

1½ Tablespoons vegetable oil

¼ onion, cut into 4 slices

3 thick slices red bell pepper

3 thick slices green bell pepper

½ medium tomato, coarsely chopped

½ teaspoon Bijol coloring, or 1 teaspoon turmeric, or 1 rounded Tablespoon *achiote* paste

¼ scant teaspoon kosher salt (adjust salt to the saltiness of the broth)

4 grinds of black pepper

1½ cups boiling Vegetable Broth (page 90) or water

1. Rinse the rice under running water until the starches run clear. Drain well, then shake the strainer to rid the rice of all moisture.

2. Heat the oil in a large saucepan (with cover). Add the onion, bell pepper, and tomato. Cook until golden. Add the rice and stir, coating the grains with oil. Continue to stir until the rice is just beginning to cook and change color.

3. Add the Bijol or turmeric, salt, and pepper to the rice. Add the hot broth, bring to a boil, cover, turn down the heat, and simmer for 25 minutes. Turn off the heat and let the rice rest for 10 minutes before removing the cover. Fluff the grains with a fork before serving.

Mexican Green Rice
Arroz Verde

Green rice gets its color from the addition of various herbs and greens. Spinach, cilantro, and flat-leaf parsley are easy-to-find greenery, yet a slew of others all work fine. Use what's at hand. You won't need much to get the right color for this special-occasion rice.

Yield: 4 servings

1 cup medium-grain white rice

2 cups Vegetable Broth (page 90) or water

1 small white onion, chopped

2 garlic cloves, chopped

¼ cup chopped flat-leaf parsley leaves

¼ cup chopped cilantro leaves

4 spinach leaves, chopped

1½ Tablespoons vegetable oil

¼ scant teaspoon kosher salt (adjust salt to the saltiness of your broth)

4 grinds of black pepper

1. Rinse the rice under running water until the starches run clear. Drain well, then shake the strainer to rid the rice of all moisture.

2. Put ¼ cup of the broth, plus the onion, garlic, parsley, cilantro, and spinach in a blender container and purée.

3. Heat the oil in a large saucepan (with cover). Add the rice and stir, coating the grains with oil until the rice is just beginning to cook and change color. Add the blender contents to the sizzling rice.

4. Meanwhile, bring the remaining broth to a boil. Add it to the rice. Add the salt and pepper. Cover, turn down the heat, and simmer for 25 minutes. Turn off the heat and let the rice sit undisturbed for 10 minutes before removing the cover. Fluff with a fork before serving.

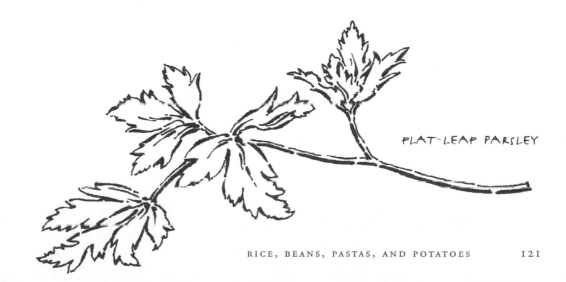

PLAT-LEAF PARSLEY

ÐOLORES GONZÁLES DE MOLENA'S

Mexican Rice and Bean Patties
Tortitas de Sobres de Arroz y Frijoles

Simple-to-make rice and bean patties are made with leftover rice—white, red, yellow, or green are all fine, and any type of leftover beans. Mexican women often cook extra to have these patties the next day. They're a lot like croquettes, but they are not deep-fried, they're panfried. Dolores's patties are fabulous served with citrusy Basic Uncooked Tomatillo Table Salsa (page 33) for taste and texture balance.

Yield: about 12 patties

½ cup vegetable oil

1 white onion, chopped

2 jalapeño chiles

1 cup cooked beans (any type)

1 cup cooked rice (white, red, yellow, or green)

½ cup crumbled *queso fresco* or shredded Monterey Jack cheese

¼ cup chopped flat-leaf parsley

½ teaspoon kosher salt

8 grinds of black pepper

2 eggs

¼ cup milk

1½ cups bread crumbs in a wide bowl

1. Heat 1 tablespoon of the oil in a skillet. Add the onion and cook until golden. Add the chiles and cook another 2 minutes.

2. In a bowl, mix the onion-chile mixture, beans, rice, cheese, parsley, salt, and pepper. Refrigerate thoroughly.

3. When cold, shape the mixture into 3-inch patties.

4. In a shallow bowl, beat the eggs with the milk. Put the breadcrumbs in another shallow bowl. Dredge each patty in the egg then coat with crumbs. Return to the refrigerator until ready to cook. The patties may be made a day in advance, wrapped in plastic.

5. Heat the remaining oil to hot in a skillet large enough to cook 4 patties at one time. Place 4 patties in the oil and cook until the bottoms are browned, about 3 minutes. Turn with a wide spatula and cook the other sides. Remove to paper towels to drain. Repeat with the remaining patties.

Drunken Beans
Frijoles Borrachos

The northern Mexican city of Monterrey is home to drunken beans. What makes these cumin-rich, mildly spiced beans so special is the use of Monterrey's claim to fame, its exemplary amber beer, Dos Equis. Feel free to use any beer available, especially if it's Mexican. Like most bean dishes, drunken beans are soupy, so do as Mexicans do and serve them in small side bowls.

Yield: 8 servings

1 pound pink or pinto beans

2 Tablespoons vegetable oil

½ cup chopped onion

½ cup chopped bell pepper

½ cup chopped mild banana or Hungarian chile, stemmed but not seeded (plus 1 or 2 spicy yellow wax chiles, if desired)

3 garlic cloves, chopped

1 Tablespoon cumin seed

3 Tablespoons ancho chile powder

8 cups water

3 Tablespoons grated piloncillo (panela), or dark brown sugar

1 bottle (12 ounces) Dos Equis

⅓ cup chopped cilantro

1 Tablespoon kosher salt

8 grinds of black pepper

1. Pick through the beans, removing any pebbles, and rinse.

2. Heat the oil in a large pot and add the onion. Sauté until the onion is transparent, then add the bell pepper, chile, garlic, cumin, and chile powder. Stir for another few minutes to lightly brown the ingredients.

3. Add the beans, water, and *piloncillo*. Bring to a boil, then reduce the heat and simmer, covered, for about 2 hours, or until the beans are barely tender.

4. Add the beer and continue to simmer, uncovered, for 20 minutes. Add the cilantro, salt, and pepper and simmer for 10 minutes longer. Taste for seasoning.

KATALINA BARRAJAS DE GÓMEZ'S

Classic Mexican Beans Cooked in a Clay Pot
Frijoles de Olla

The traditional way to cook beans in Mexico is in an earthenware pot called an *olla*. The pot sits directly on a bed of charcoal, smoldering wood, or on a stove's back burner, where the beans bubble away until done. Whether *veracruzanos* (tiny black); *flor de mayo* (splotchy purple); *canarios* (gold); *bayos* or *sabinos* (dark tan); *aluvias* or *ibes* (white); *habas* (large green and white); *peruano* (very light pinky-gold); *mayo* or *junio* (tiny pink beans picked in May or June that look like small pinto beans); or countless other varieties, Mexican beans are served brothy and alongside (or after) the main course in separate, small bowls. Often salt and an onion is the only flavoring. Sometimes a regional chile, garlic clove, or a few sprigs of cilantro or *epazote* are added for variation. Fresh lime juice makes black beans sing out with flavor.

Mexicans don't presoak beans because they know that so much of that good bean taste is lost with presoaking, especially if the water is changed. Any time that presoaking saves really isn't worth the flavor loss (to say nothing of color loss in black beans). If you insist, bring water to a boil and cook the dried beans for 2 minutes. Remove the pot from the heat and soak the beans for 2 hours before continuing. Do not replace the water. People say replacing this flavorful liquid with fresh water diminishes gas-causing substances. I have never noticed any difference except flavor loss. The best way to speed cooking time is to always cover the beanpot. Bean cooking time depends on the age and size of the beans. Recently harvested beans may take less than 30 minutes, while ancient specimens found in the back of your pantry may take 4 hours. To avoid dry or cracked beans, be sure liquid always covers the beans while they cook. Mexican beans are always soupy—so much so that they're served in side bowls rather than on a plate. It's been said by many people that salting toughens uncooked beans, so don't season until the beans are completely finished and ready to serve.

Yield: 8 servings, 7 to 8 cups

1 pound dried beans (about
 2½ cups)
1 white onion, halved
2 teaspoons kosher salt
1 lime, juiced

1. Pick over the beans and discard any pebbles. Rinse. Put the beans and onion in a nonreactive pot and add boiling water to cover by 2 inches (or 3 times the bean volume, whatever method is easier).

2. Bring to a boil, then reduce the heat and cook at a very low simmer for 1½ to 2 hours, covered, until the beans are soft. Time depends on the type, size, and age of the beans.

3. Add salt and lime juice just before serving. Taste for seasoning. Beans, like many stews and soups, taste better the next day. Cool the beans and refrigerate because they can sour if left at room temperature. Cooked beans may be frozen.

Note: You may also slow-cook beans in a 250°F oven for about 12 hours, checking the water level regularly. Beans also turn out just fine when cooked in an electric slow cooker: Put the beans, water, and an onion in a pot and cook for about 12 hours. Or, if more convenient, cook on high for 1 hour, then turn to low and cook for about 8 hours.

CLAY BEAN POT

Refried Beans
Frijoles Refritos

Mexico's glorious refried beans are Classic Mexican Beans Cooked in a Clay Pot (page 124), mashed and loaded with lard. They can easily be made with minimal butter or vegetable oil, or without fat altogether with the use of a nonstick skillet. On the other hand, refried beans are an out-of-this-world experience when made with olive oil. When Katalina and I cooked up a pot of *frijoles refritos,* made with pinto beans and fruity olive oil, we couldn't believe how blissful a plate of beans could be.

Yield: 8 servings

**Butter, vegetable oil, or
   olive oil**
***Frijoles de Olla* (page 124)**
**Salt and freshly ground
   pepper**

1. Heat 3 tablespoons butter or oil in a heavy skillet over medium heat (or use a heavy nonstick pan). Add about 2 cups of the beans, including some broth. Mash the beans into the fat with a bean or potato masher. The broth will reduce and the beans will dry.

2. Add a cup at a time of the remaining beans and broth, and as much additional fat as you want, mashing constantly until a coarse purée is achieved. Total mashing time is about 10 minutes. Taste for seasoning, adding salt and pepper if necessary. *Frijoles refritos* thicken as soon as the skillet is removed from the heat. The beans may be cooled, refrigerated, and served the next day reheated with more fat. *Frijoles refritos* also freeze well—defrost, then reheat in additional oil.

Variation: Heat vegetable oil and saute 1 large white onion, chopped. Stir in ½ cup (or to taste) canned, pickled jalapeños, chopped. Mix into the refried beans.

WOODEN SPOON AND BEAN MASHER

Refried Black Beans with Sweetened Smoky, Spicy Chile
Frijoles Negros Refritos

A spectacular combination of sweet molasses-flavored black beans and smoky chiles is from the southern region of the state of Veracruz. Juanita's very thick, somewhat lumpy bean spread is wonderful spooned onto warm tortillas, or scooped with corn chips and squirted with fresh lime juice. Maybe Juanita's bougainvillea-filled courtyard lit by a full moon helps, but a lively group of her friends concluded one balmy evening that her refried black beans and Sangría Preparada (page 181) make a mighty fine combination. Later a group of my recipe taste testers unconditionally agreed.

Yield: 8 servings

1 recipe Frijoles Refritos (page 126) made with black beans

2 *chiles chipotles en adobo,* finely chopped

4 ounces *piloncillo (panela)* melted with some bean liquid, or ½ cup dark brown sugar

Juice of 1 lime

⅓ cup crumbled queso fresca, dry farmer cheese, or mild feta cheese (optional)

1. Heat the *frijoles refritos* in a very large skillet with the chipotle chiles and *piloncillo,* stirring until the sugar is melted and the paste very thick.

2. Stir in the lime juice. The beans thicken when you remove them from the heat. Serve sprinkled with the optional cheese.

Variation: With either Refried Beans (page 126) or refried black beans, you can easily make bean patties. If using refried beans: Sauté 1 teaspoon cumin seed with 1 chopped onion and mix into the beans. Form the beans into 3-inch patties (half size for hors d'oeuvres), and roll in bread crumbs. Refrigerate until cold. Panfry in vegetable oil. Top with chunky tomato salsa and a dollop of *Crema* (page 49) or sour cream.

Pasta Pancake
Sopa Seca de Fideos

Isaac has owned Galeria Atenea, an art gallery in picture-postcard-perfect San Miguel de Allende, for over ten years. He was brought up in nearby Irapuato, and remembers this dish fondly from his youth. Firm, non-mushy *sopa seca de fideos,* made with pasta, is real Mexican home cooking. You'll never see *sopa seca* like this at a restaurant. Restaurant-style *sopa seca de fideos* is most often served during *comida,* the large afternoon meal, as a soft pasta dish before the entrée. Isaac enjoys his family's crisp, dry *sopa seca de fideos,* along with a cold cucumber salad, when he has a hankering for a light, healthful meal.

Yield: 4 servings

¼ cup plus 1 Tablespoon vegetable oil

8 ounces fideo pasta nests

1 medium onion, chopped

2 garlic cloves, chopped

1 jalapeño chile, stemmed, seeded, and chopped

8 small to medium tomatoes, chopped

1 Tablespoon dried Mexican oregano

½ teaspoon kosher salt

4 grinds of black pepper

½ cup dry wine if the tomatoes are dry (optional)

½ cup crumbled queso fresca, dry farmer cheese, or mild feta cheese

2 Tablespoons chopped flat-leaf parsley or cilantro

1. Heat the ¼ cup oil in a small, 6-inch skillet. When the oil is hot, carefully place one pasta nest in the center. Cook for about 30 seconds, until golden brown, and turn over to cook the other side. Remove to paper towels to drain. Continue with the remaining pasta nests.

2. In a large skillet that can be put under a broiler, heat the 1 tablespoon vegetable oil. Add the onion and cook until it is transparent. Add the garlic and chile and cook until golden. Add the tomatoes with their juice, oregano, salt, pepper, and optional wine. Turn down the heat, cover, and simmer for 20 minutes.

3. Add the pasta to the sauce and stir, breaking up the pasta. Cover the skillet and simmer for another 15 minutes. The pasta absorbs all the sauce and becomes firm, like a large pancake. Continue cooking longer if you want the bottom to be crisp, as Isaac does.

4. Cover the entire top with the cheese. Isaac likes to run the skillet under a broiler to melt the cheese and crisp the top. He says browning the cheese isn't necessary; it's not done at home because most people don't have broilers.

Home Fries with Onions and Chile Powder
Papas con Cebollas y Chile

A fast, favorite side dish, red potatoes with chile powder, is made everywhere in Mexico with the country's especially sweet red potatoes. The dish takes on a terracotta cast from the chile powder. Be generous and put extra chile in the skillet because the mixture should be a little spicy when served with simple vegetables. Sprinkle with fresh lime juice just before serving. *Papas con Cebollas y Chile* makes an omelet filling fit for Aztec gods. *Yield: 4 servings*

4 medium-size red potatoes,
   cut into quarters

3 Tablespoons vegetable oil

1 large white onion, sliced

4 garlic cloves, chopped

Chile powder to taste,
   depending on the type
   of chile

1 teaspoon kosher salt

4 grinds of black pepper

3 chopped *epazote* leaves
   (optional)

1 lime

1. Bring salted water to a boil in a pot and cook the potatoes for 20 minutes, or until they are tender. Drain. Cool enough to handle and peel. Cut each quarter into a few thick slices.

2. Heat the oil in a large skillet and add the potatoes and onion. Turn with a spatula until the vegetables are pale gold. Add the garlic and cook until the garlic turns golden. Add the chile powder, salt, pepper, and *epazote*. Cook, stirring to coat the potatoes and lightly toast the chile powder. Sprinkle with lime juice just before serving.

Meatless Main Dishes

YOU WON'T SEE ANY OVER-SPICY, OVER-GREASY, FAKE MEXICAN
food around here. Mexico's authentic, captivating dishes aren't even similar to
those heartburn jump-starters you eat at that corner greasy spoon. There's not
a prepared or frozen product in sight—what *is* here are fresh foods made with
quality ingredients that produce memorable meals. Also, look in the Soups
chapter and serve big bowls as hearty main courses; a few *antojitos* or tamales translates into main dishes; and don't forget all the exciting Mexican egg dishes. *Verduras
Pibil,* a hearty plate of winter vegetables rubbed with a seasoning paste and baked in
banana leaves; the fluffiest, crispiest *Chiles Rellenos* anyone was ever fortunate enough
to sink a fork into; and a big pan of *Chilaquiles,* a Mexican lasagne that will force
everyone at your next party to sit up and take notice, are a few temptations.

Cactus Paddles Cooked with Onion, Tomatoes, and Chiles
Sopa Seca de Nopales

Soledad, owner of Oaxaca's El Topil restaurant (see page 214), shocked me when she said that all vegetables not cooked in liquid are called *sopa seca*. I always thought *sopa seca* was a term for "dry soup," to differentiate between rice and pastas cooked until the liquid is completely absorbed by the starch, and *sopa* (soup) where rice or pasta is added to broth and eaten with a spoon. But here's the truth: Any vegetable cooked and served without the cooking liquid is called *sopa seca* in Mexico. A vegetable served in a simple broth, as a soup, is called *sopa aguada* or *sopa caldosa*. Here's the typical Mexican dry soup of any vegetable. Use it as a basic recipe and experiment.

Opuntia plants are native to almost every state in Mexico. You see the huge, dangerous-looking cactus when driving through wilderness areas, as well as neat rows of cultivated farm specimens. People pick wild paddles and their fruit, the prickly pear *(tuna,* in Spanish), is deliciously sweet. Red or green, pricker-covered fruits are about the size and shape of extra-large eggs. The *nopales* (paddles) are oval, deep green, fleshy disks covered with needlelike spikes that can be painfully sharp. Sizes vary from too big (12 x 8 x ½ inch thick monsters) to *nopalitos* (tiny, delicate babies 4 x 2 x ⅛ inch thick). *Nopalitos* are used for salads and vegetable dishes, while the large paddles are boiled for gelatinous soups chosen by people who enjoy the texture, which is similar to that of okra.

Even though *nopales* may be Mexico's most popular vegetable next to corn, supermarkets here rarely offer them fresh. Water-packed in jars, *nopales* are typical shelf items. Forget anything canned. Look in Latino markets for fresh—any extra effort will be worth your trouble. Fresh *nopales* (and prickly pears) are sold with their needles scraped off. Tackling this lousy job is plainly not worth the grief, but be sure to scrape off any straggling needles before trimming. To trim, cut off the tough base end, then trim the outer edge around the circumference. With a heavy knife, scrape off the bumps where the needles grew out of the paddle—on both sides—but do not remove the entire skin.

The slimy texture of *nopales* needs to be dealt with. Tips from a few pros: Daniela van Beuren of Mexico City's Fonda El Refugio restaurant says to cook *nopales* in an unlined copper pot because copper keeps them from oozing; other chefs drop cleaned copper pennies into their cooking water; Reyna Polanca Abrahams (page 213) instructs students to rinse *nopales* thoroughly after boiling; and in the U.S., Austin's Jay McCarthy (a.k.a. the Internet's Cactus King) swears that harvesting paddles in early morning hours, rather than later in the day when hot sun has been beating down on them, is the only way to go.

Yield: 4 servings

1 pound small nopales paddles, cleaned and trimmed (they are used interchangably with green beans in Mexico so feel free to substitute beans trimmed to the same size)

½ white onion

2 Tablespoons vegetable oil

1 medium white onion, chopped

2 garlic cloves, chopped

2 jalapeño chiles, stemmed, seeded, and chopped

2 plum tomatoes, chopped

3 Tablespoons chopped *epazote* or cilantro

1. Cut the paddles into 2-inch strips at ¼-inch width. Boil in 3 quarts boiling, salted water with the piece of onion for 5 minutes and drain. Run cold water over the *nopales* to eliminate their slimy texture. Bring another 3 quarts water to a boil and return the *nopales* to the boiling water for 10 minutes, until tender. Drain. If not serving immediately, run cold water over them to stop the cooking process.

2. To cook *nopales* with an onion-chile mixture: Heat the oil in a skillet. Add the chopped onion and sauté until transparent. Add the garlic and chiles, cooking and stirring until golden. Add the tomatoes and cook for 10 minutes. Add the cooked *nopales* and cilantro and heat through.

Variations: For *nopales* soup, make the *nopales* mixture in a large pot rather than a skillet. Add 4 cups Vegetable Broth (page 90) and bring to a boil. Turn down the heat and simmer for 20 minutes. Adjust seasonings. Top each bowl of soup with fresh cilantro and queso añejo or Parmesan cheese.

For *nopales* salad, make the *nopales* mixture, cool, then refrigerate. In a small bowl, mix 4 Tablespoons olive oil with 1 teaspoon prepared mustard. Add ½ teaspoon sugar and continue to mix until the sugar dissolves. Add ½ teaspoon kosher salt and a generous grinding of pepper. Add 1 Tablespoon lime juice or vinegar and mix. Stir the *nopales* with vinaigrette and adjust seasoning. Spoon onto plates and top with raw onion rings and a crumbled queso fresco such as ranchero, or mild feta cheese.

Grilled Corn on the Cob
Elotes

Grilled corn is one of Mexico's favorite street foods. And what street food! After waiting on an inevitable line (where the aroma makes you faint from hunger) the cook finally grabs an ear of large, chewy corn, rubs a chile-dipped lime wedge all over it, and hands it over, on a fresh corn leaf "plate." You can easily make a meal from one of these big beauties. An added gift: You'll never miss gobs of butter and salt on corn on the cob again.

Yield: 4 servings

4 ears of corn, leaves and silk removed, reserving 8 of the largest leaves, washed

2 Tablespoons kosher salt

1 lime, quartered

2 Tablespoons chile powder on a small plate

1. Place the ears of corn on a medium-hot grill. Turn the ears until the corn is cooked and small areas begin to brown and blacken.

2. Dissolve the salt in 1 gallon of hot water. Dip each ear of corn into the salted water just before serving.

3. Dip a lime quarter in chile powder and rub the powder and juice over the corn ear. Repeat with the remaining corn. Place each ear on a 2-leaf "plate."

CORN ON THE COB

Fresh Corn Patties
Croquetitas de Maíz

Rosa's recipe is from her Mexico City gourmet club's inventory of recipes. When we were scanning her looseleaf book for interesting meatless dishes, she squealed with delight when the page was turned to this recipe made by her sister, Carmita, for a club get-together. One patty of this easy and tempting recipe can be served as an appetizer. A larger portion can be a main course. Rosa serves these fresh corn patties with chunky Basic Uncooked Tomatillo Table Salsa, (page 33) and garnishes the dish with a few cilantro sprigs and a bit of *Crema* (page 49).

Yield: about 12 patties, depending on size

2 ancho chiles

1 cup coarse *masa harina* (for tamales)

¾ cup water

2 eggs, lightly beaten

3 ears of corn

¼ cup chopped cilantro

1 teaspoon sugar

2 teaspoons kosher salt

8 grinds of black pepper

1 Tablespoon vegetable oil (plus extra)

1. Soak the chiles in hot water for 30 minutes to soften.

2. In a large bowl, mix the *masa harina* and ½ cup of the water to form a dough. Add the eggs and additional water and mix until you get a moist, sticky dough.

3. Stem, seed, then finely chop the soaked chiles and mix them into the dough.

4. Remove the leaves and silk from the corn. Scrape the kernels into a large bowl. Add the kernels to the dough and mix with the cilantro, sugar, salt, and pepper. Mix well.

5. In a large nonstick skillet, heat the oil over high heat. Oil your hands and shape the sticky dough into 2-inch patties about ¼ inch thick. Slip as many patties into the hot skillet as fit comfortably. Brown to crisp on both sides, turn the heat down, and cook over low heat for 20 minutes. The dough inside needs to be completely cooked or it tastes raw. You may want to use two skillets to make the cooking go faster; otherwise, keep the patties in a warm oven while preparing the second batch.

Purslane with Potatoes in Green Sauce
Verdolagas con Papas en Salsa de Tomatillo

Purslane *(Purslane oleracea)* arrived via Spain during the 1670s but may be difficult to find in your area (look in local farmer's markets and health food stores during summer months) but don't fret. Isaac says this dish is also delicious made with slightly spicy/bitter watercress. Purslane with Potatoes in Green Sauce is home-style cooking favored in the state of Guanajuato, where Isaac lives. Wrap warm corn or flour tortillas around the mixture for soft tacos, or serve on a plate with rice pilaf.

Yield: 4 servings

4 medium-size red potatoes,
   quartered

1 pound tomatillos

3 Tablespoons vegetable oil

1 large onion, coarsely
   chopped

3 garlic cloves, chopped

3 serrano chiles, stemmed and
   chopped

3 thick onion slices, about
   ¼ inch

1 pound purslane, all thick
   stems removed

¼ cup chopped cilantro leaves

½ teaspoon kosher salt

8 grinds of black pepper

1. Bring salted water to a boil in a pot (nonstick is best) and cook the potatoes until they are tender, about 20 minutes. Drain the water and cool the potatoes enough to handle, then peel. Dice into ½-inch cubes.

2. Meanwhile, add more water to the pot and bring it to a boil. Remove the papery husks and boil the tomatillos until they change color, about 8 minutes. Drain and cool the tomatillos for 20 minutes. Isaac says this cooling step helps remove acidity from the tomatillos.

3. Add 1 tablespoon oil to the same pot and sauté the chopped onion until transparent. Add the garlic and chiles and sauté until golden. Put the onion mixture in a blender with the tomatillos and purée.

4. In the pot, heat the remaining 2 tablespoons oil and sauté the potatoes with the onion slices until golden. Add the green salsa, cilantro, salt, and pepper and cook for 5 minutes. Add the purslane and cook for 2 minutes.

PURSLANE

Stuffed Chayote Squash
Chayotes Rellenos

Chayote squash is also known as *mirliton* in the South, and as *christophene* in the Caribbean and France. The green, pear-shaped summer squash is so mild that it takes on the flavor of anything cooked with it. Use medium to large unpeeled chayote for this recipe so that the firm squash can hold lots of savory stuffing. Francisca, like most Mexicans, makes stuffed squash when she has leftover rice and tomato sauce.

Yield: 4 servings

2 guajillo or ancho chiles

2 de árbol chiles, or any tiny, hot, dried chile (if you want the stuffing slightly spicy)

2 chayote squash (about 10 ounces each)

½ teaspoon kosher salt

8 grinds of black pepper

1¼ cups shredded quesillo de Oaxaca, mozzarella, or Monterey Jack cheese

2 cups any leftover cooked rice, reheated

2 cups Basic Cooked Tomato Sauce (page 32)

¼ cup chopped flat-leaf parsley

1. Preheat the oven to 375°F.

2. Soak the chiles in a bowl of hot water for at least 30 minutes. Stem, seed, and chop fine.

3. Bring a pot of salted water to a boil. Add the chayotes and cook for 20 to 25 minutes, or until tender. Drain well. When the chayotes are cool enough to handle, cut in half horizontally and remove the seed. Scoop out and reserve the pulp, leaving ¼-inch shells. Sprinkle the shells with salt and pepper. Chop the reserved pulp.

4. Mix the minced chiles with 1 cup of the shredded cheese, the chopped chayote, and rice.

5. Mound a quarter of the mixture on each chayote half, forming a dome shape. Arrange the stuffed shells in a baking dish. Pour the tomato sauce around the squash. Sprinkle with the remaining ¼ cup cheese, cover, and bake for 35 minutes. Remove the cover and bake for 10 minutes, until heated through and the cheese is brown and bubbling. Spoon tomato sauce from the dish around the chayotes, sprinkle with parsley, and serve.

ROSARIO CHÁVEZ'S

Vegetables Baked in Banana Leaves
Verdura Pibil

Pibil, Yucatán's most famous dish, is usually made with either pork or chicken, and flavored with a *recado* (seasoning paste), before being wrapped in banana leaves and lowered into a pit for slow underground cooking. Rosario generously rubs paste over vegetables, then wraps them in banana leaves before baking in her home oven for this fabulously flavored low-fat meal. You can buy huge, fresh banana leaves in Latino or Filipino markets. Frozen or dried leaves are available in many Asian markets. Rosario says to serve *pibil* with Yucatecan accompaniments of puréed black beans, yellow rice, and *Cebolla Curdita* (page 157). She offers *pibil* with *Panuchos* (page 67) to her guests on special occasions.
Yield: 8 servings

8 carrots, peeled and cut in thirds

3 medium yams, peeled and quartered

8 small turnips, peeled and quartered

5 summer squash, such as chayote, zucchini, or pattypan, quartered

1 winter squash, such as acorn or butternut, peeled, seeded, and cut into large chunks

½ cup *recado rojo* or *achiote* paste

1 teaspoon kosher salt

½ cup orange juice

2 limes, juiced

1 Tablespoon vegetable oil

1. Preheat the oven to 350°F.

2. Put the prepared vegetables in a large bowl. In a small bowl, combine the seasoning paste, salt, orange juice, lime juice, and oil. Spread the mixture over the vegetables.

3. Roughly line a large Dutch oven, stockpot that fits into your oven, or roasting pan with 2 large banana leaves (about 2 feet x 5 feet), leaving some overlapping the sides. If the leaves are very thick and brittle, boil them for 1 minute to soften. You may also singe them on both sides over a gas burner to soften. Place the vegetables over the leaves.

4. Spread the onions and tomatoes over the vegetables. Nestle one whole habanero chile in the center of the pot to be removed at the end of cooking (be sure the chile is not cut open or your entire pot of *pibil* could be too spicy). Place another banana leaf on top and tuck the leaves around the vegetables to seal in all the flavors.

5. Cover the pot tightly (or use foil on a roasting pan) and bake for 2 hours. Remove the top layer of banana leaves and discard. Remove the habanero chile and set it aside. Remove

3 banana leaves, washed, with their nonpliable center ribs cut away

2 white onions, thickly sliced

3 tomatoes, thickly sliced

2 habanero chiles

the vegetables to a large platter or bowl. Discard the remaining banana leaves. Rosario cuts the remaining habanero chile in half and places it in a small dish with the baked chile. People who enjoy spice wipe a tortilla over the cut chile for a little of its heat and unique flavor. Chileheads take a piece of either the cooked or raw habanero chile to eat along with their vegetables.

BANANA LEAVES

Cheese-Stuffed Chiles, Battered and Fried
Chiles Rellenos

Since *A Cook's Tour of Mexico* was published, I had an impromptu cooking lesson one night in Oaxaca while watching Soledad cook in her restaurant, El Topíl (page 214). A few pointers she casually shared have convinced me to adjust my *chiles rellenos* recipes from now on—such as to drain the chiles on screening rather than on paper towels. Her marvelous cooking techniques produce huge, fluffy, crisp, grease-free *rellenos* guaranteed to be your favorite new dish when exciting flavors are on tap for a fun evening of Mexican good eats. Surround each chile with a few spoonfuls of Basic Cooked Tomato Sauce (page 32). *Yield: 12 stuffed chiles*

12 poblano chiles, stems attached (you may substitute Anaheim chilies; Soledad uses spicy de agua chiles available only in Oaxaca)

3 cups cubed quesillo de Oaxaca, mozzarella, or Monterey Jack cheese

4 eggs, separated (whites in a large bowl), plus additional eggs if needed

1 teaspoon fresh lime juice in the egg whites (Soledad's hint to keep them stiff) if you are refrigerating the *rellenos* to serve within 3 days, plus additional if needed

1 cup flour, plus additional if needed

Special equipment: Soledad uses an ingenious system to drain her chiles: She has a 12 x 20-inch piece of screening (as for windows) set over a metal pan on which she places just-fried *rellenos*. This works better than draining on paper towels because the *rellenos* never have the chance to resoak their own oil.

1. Preheat the broiler. To blister this many chiles it's easiest to arrange them on a baking sheet and put the sheet under a very hot broiler. Turn after 1 minute, turn again after 1 minute, etc., until the chile skins have been *completely* charred—black all over. Place the chiles in a plastic bag so they can "sweat," then peel the skins.

2. Cut a slit down the side of each from just under the stem area to a ½ inch above the bottom pointed end. Gently open the chile and scrape out the seeds with a teaspoon, keeping the stem intact. Be sure to get all the seeds from the hard area under the stem. Remove the veins running vertically along the inside wall. Pat dry.

3. Stuff each chile with ¼ cup cheese, pressing the cheese

1 cup vegetable oil, plus enough to maintain a ⅛-inch depth in the skillet

into the chile firmly and slightly overlapping the sides of the chile to envelop the cheese.

4. Beat the egg whites (with lime juice, if using) until soft peaks form. Add the yolks and continue to beat until stiff peaks form. Sprinkle ¼ cup of the flour over the beaten eggs and beat for 10 seconds more to incorporate.

5. Heat the oil in a 10-inch skillet to hot (375°F).

6. Spread the remaining ¾ cup flour on a plate for coating the chiles. Roll a chile in the flour, pat off, then put it on a plate. Using a large spoon, scoop some egg batter on top of the chile. Turn the chile over and cover with more egg. Spoon even more batter on top.

7. Soledad cooks only one *relleno* at a time. Take the plate over to the skillet and carefully place the *relleno* in the center of the hot oil with the help of a metal spatula. With the spatula, splatter droplets of hot oil onto the top of the *relleno* in quick motions. The batter will puff. When the bottom is golden, after about 1 minute, turn the *relleno* on its side with the spatula and cook, holding it in place, for 5 seconds (Soledad says that this step ensures a thick, compact shape). Turn the *relleno* over and continue to cook until the second side is golden brown.

8. Remove the *relleno* and place it on the piece of screening over the pan, or place it on layers of paper towels, changing the paper towels after 5 minutes so the batter doesn't reabsorb oil from saturated towels. Continue with the remaining chiles, preparing additional egg batter if needed. Add additional oil to the skillet, if necessary, heating it before adding another chile. Cooked *chiles rellenos* may be reheated. They also may be refrigerated (include lime juice in the batter) for up to 3 days and reheated in hot oil.

(Continued)

Variations:

Cheese and Grilled Vegetable-Stuffed Chiles

Stir together a selection of grilled and chopped vegetables
(2 cups total) with 2 cups shredded cheese. Continue with
the recipe as above. Chiles are also delicious stuffed with an
equal mixture of cheese and highly seasoned cooked
black beans.

Stuffed Ancho Chiles

Simmer 12 dried ancho chiles in 2 quarts water with 1½ cups
piloncillo (panela) for 30 minutes. Continue with the recipe
as above. Or, for a healthful alternative, stuffed chiles
are often not battered and fried but baked at 375°F until the
cheese melts. Serve with rice and Basic Cooked Tomato
Sauce (page 32).

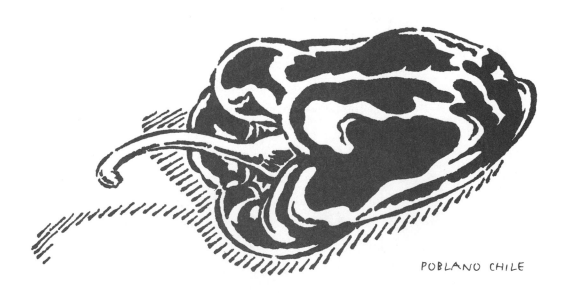

POBLANO CHILE

Fried Tortillas Cooked in Salsa
Chilaquiles

Juan, a tour guide in Oaxaca City, told me he has two easy dishes he prepares on those occasions when his wife or mother-in-law (better cooks than himself) are busy. One is *Rajas* (page 145) to load onto warm tortillas, the other is the Mexican *fonda* masterpiece, *chilaquiles,* made from stale tortillas cooked in a skillet with either tomato or tomatillo sauce, depending on what's in the pantry. Juan insists that the tortillas for his *chilaquiles* are torn into irregular pieces—other cooks throughout Mexico cut tortillas into triangles or strips. For a very home-style breakfast, lunch, or light supper, it's hard to beat *chilaquiles* because everyone loves the dish any time of day.

Yield: 4 servings

1½ cups vegetable oil

8 stale corn tortillas

2 cups (½ recipe) Basic Cooked
   Tomatillo Sauce (page 34)
   or Basic Cooked Tomato
   Sauce (page 32)

¼ cup queso fresco, dry
   cottage cheese, or farmer
   cheese

1 large slice white onion

1 sprig *epazote* (optional)

1. Heat the oil in a deep skillet or pot. Tear the tortillas (Juan says definitely do not cut) and drop them into the hot oil. Cook, stirring, until the tortillas are very crisp and their color is darker. Drain on paper towels. Drain the oil from the skillet.

2. Return the tortillas to the skillet and add the sauce. Stir, then cook until the tortillas have absorbed some sauce and have begun to get soft. A chewy tortilla texture is mandatory for all *chilaquiles.*

3. Spoon onto plates and sprinkle with cheese. Top each with a few onion rings. If you really like *epazote,* as Juan does, chop a few leaves and sprinkle over the onion slices.

Baked Tortilla-Chile Casserole
Chilaquiles

Baked *chilaquiles* (different from Fried Tortillas Cooked in Salsa, page 143), is the perfect party dish—a Mexican lasagne for a crowd. *Chilaquiles* is one of the most famous breakfast dishes in Mexico, so it could easily be your main dish for a special brunch. Serve it with two or more table salsas, a fresh green salad, and jícama sticks sprinkled with lime juice and chile powder. This recipe can be doubled easily and baked in one huge, or two medium casseroles.

Yield: 12 serving

48 stale corn tortillas, at least 2 days old (or dried in the oven)

1 to 2 cups vegetable oil

Basic Cooked Tomato Sauce (page 32) made with *chiles chipotles en adobo*

1 cup shredded quesillo de Oaxaca, mozzarella, or Monterey Jack cheese

2 heaping Tablespoons dried Mexican oregano

1 cup crumbled *queso fresco* such as ranchero, or farmer, or dry cottage cheese

2 cups Crema (page 49) or sour cream (optional)

1. Preheat oven to 375°F.

2. Stack some of the tortillas and cut through them into sixths (pie style). Continue with the rest. Heat the oil in a large skillet, fry the tortilla pieces, and drain them on paper towels. They must remain chewy in the sauce so don't let them get too crisp—chewiness is essential to this dish.

3. Mix the tortilla chips, tomato sauce, shredded cheese, and dried oregano.

4. Immediately pour the mixture into a greased shallow casserole and bake for about 35 minutes, until browned and bubbly. Scoop onto plates, topping each portion with some crumbled cheese and a spoonful of *crema* or sour cream.

Variation: Prepare *chilaquiles* with Basic Cooked Tomatillo Sauce (page 34) for a delectable, traditional change.

DOÑA ESPERANZA DE SEPULVEDA'S
Baked Layered Tortilla-Chile Casserole
Pastel del Pobres

Pastel del Pobres translates to "cake of the poor"—rich or poor, this version of baked *chilaquiles* is a luscious lasagne made with whole corn tortillas rather than pasta sheets. Similar to Baked Chilaquiles (page 144), the casserole is an ideal party dish. Esperancita (a nickname for Esperanza) includes layers of *rajas* made with mild poblano chiles, for interest. She lives in the highlands of Michoacán, where the food is generally not spicy. When she wants to add heat to any dish or meal, Esperancita makes a fresh table salsa with chopped perón (a.k.a. manzano) chiles, onion, cilantro, and orange juice.

Yield: 8 servings

For the rajas:

3 poblano chiles

1 large white onion

1 Tablespoon vegetable oil

1. Toast (page 28) the poblano chiles, sweat them in a plastic bag, peel, stem, and seed. Slice into vertical strips, about ¼ inch wide. Cut the onion vertically into ¼-inch slices.

2. Heat the oil and cook the onion until it is golden. Add the chiles and simmer 3 minutes.

6 large ripe tomatoes

1 large white onion, chopped

4 jalapeño chiles, stemmed

8 garlic cloves

4 Tablespoons butter

½ teaspoon kosher salt

5 poblano chiles

1 cup vegetable oil

24 stale corn tortillas

2 cups Crema (page 49) or crème fraîche

1 cup grated queso anejo or Parmesan cheese

1. Core the tomatoes and put them in a blender with the chopped onion, the jalapeño chiles, and the garlic. Purée.

2. Heat 2 tablespoons of the butter in a pot, add the purée and the salt, and cook for 20 minutes, uncovered.

3. Preheat the oven to 375°F. Generously grease a large, shallow casserole with the remaining butter.

4. Heat the vegetable oil in a deep skillet to 370°F. Pass each tortilla quickly through the oil, about 5 seconds. Drain the tortillas on paper towels, patting out any remaining oil.

5. Arrange a layer of the tortillas on the bottom of the casserole. Spread ½ cup sauce over the tortillas. Spread ½ cup *crema* over the sauce. Scatter on some of the dry cheese. Add strips of *rajas* across the cheese. Continue with alternating layers, ending with a layer of *rajas* sprinkled with cheese. Bake for 15 minutes, or until the top is bubbling and golden.

PILAR CABRERA'S

Golden Cauliflower Fritters
Coliflor Rellenos en Salsa Roja

Pilar, owner of Oaxaca's Café de Olla (page 214), prepares this favorite family-style recipe at her minuscule café. The dish (whether at her café or at your house) will make you feel that you are eating in her home kitchen. The four-table *fonda (fonda,* in the true sense of the word, because it's attached to the front of the family house) gets many of its recipes for the daily *comida* from Pilar's mother and grandmother, two of Oaxaca's premier home cooks. Serve the cauliflower fritters surrounded with Basic Cooked Tomato Sauce (page 32) made with generous quantities of fresh jalapeño or serrano chile.

Yield: 6 servings

1 large head cauliflower

1 cup crumbled queso panela, ranchero, or dry farmer cheese

1 teaspoon kosher salt

8 grinds of black pepper

3 eggs, separated, additional if needed

1 cup flour, additional if needed

1 cup vegetable oil, plus enough to maintain a ⅛-inch depth in the skillet

Basic Cooked Tomato Sauce (page 32)

1. Break cauliflower into florets and steam until tender.

2. Mash the cauliflower with the cheese, salt, and pepper, leaving some lumps.

3. Beat the egg whites in another bowl. Slowly add the yolks, beating in slowly. Sprinkle a tablespoon of flour over the egg batter and fold in.

4. Heat the oil in a large skillet to 375°F.

5. Spread the remaining ¾ cup flour on a dish for coating the fritters. Form fritters with the cauliflower mixture and roll in the flour. Shake off excess. Put a fritter on a plate and scoop some egg batter on top. Turn the fritter over and cover with more egg. Spoon even more batter on top.

6. Cook only 2 or 3 fritters at a time. Take the plate over to the skillet and carefully place the fritters in the hot oil with the help of a metal spatula. With the spatula, splatter droplets of hot oil onto the top of the fritters in quick motions. The batter will puff. When the bottoms are golden, turn the fritters over and continue to cook until the second sides are golden.

7. Remove the fritters and place them on the piece of screening over the pan (see page 140), or layers of paper towels, changing the towels after 5 minutes to keep the fritters from reabsorbing the oil from the saturated towels. Continue with the remaining fritters. Prepare additional egg batter, if needed, and add additional oil to the skillet if necessary, heating it to 375°F before adding more fritters. Cooked fritters may be reheated or refrigerated for up to 3 days and reheated in hot oil (lower temperature oil makes for greasy fritters).

RIPE RED TOMATOES

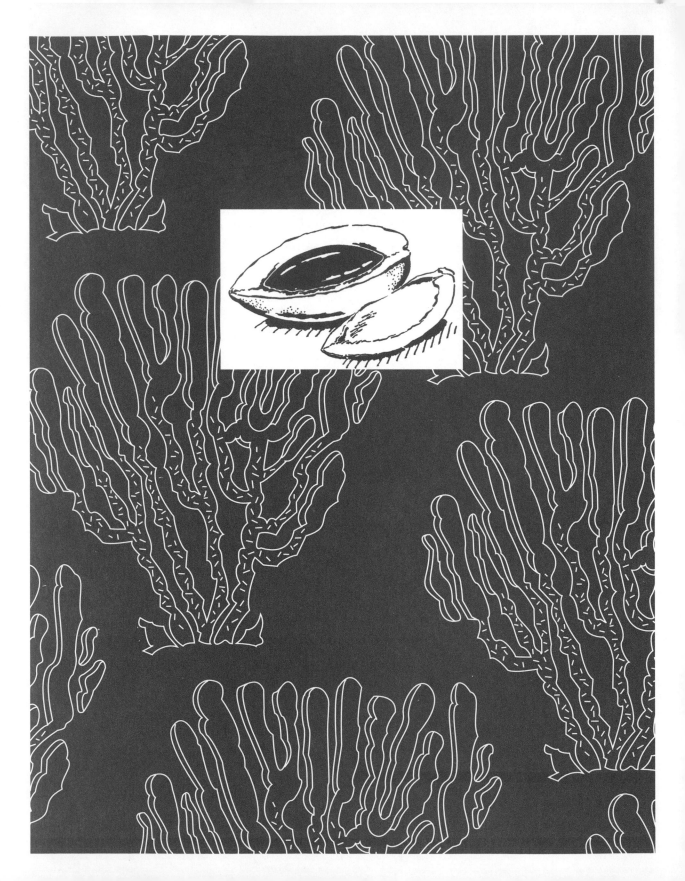

Egg Dishes

MEXICAN EGG YOLKS ARE THE COLOR OF A KODAK FILM BOX because backyard chickens run free and pick at their organic food, and chickens are fed marigold flowers that have been mixed into their feed. Mexicans love eggs and eat them with gusto anytime during the day. Mexican breakfast egg dishes are legendary; midday *comida* often includes an egg poached in vegetable broth, or a fried egg placed over rice; and a light supper of scrambled eggs with sautéed chiles and onions stuffed into warm tortillas sure hits the spot. Chile-sauced *Huevos Rancheros* are synonymous with late breakfasts on sun-filled patios; *Tortilla Español,* a frittata of browned potatoes and caramelized onions held together with eggs, is a superb buffet dish; or *Papadzules,* Yucatán treats made with hard-boiled eggs, rolled in corn tortillas and embellished with tomato and pumpkin seed sauces, sound more difficult to make than they are.

Scrambled Eggs with Fabulous Flavors
Huevos Mexicanos

Fresh ingredients, simply cooked and generously seasoned, are hallmarks of Mexican home cooking. A plate of scrambled eggs with sautéed vegetables, chiles, and herbs is good food that anyone can whip up in no time. For an almost instant meal, pass a basket filled with warm tortillas.

Yield: 4 servings

2 Tablespoons vegetable oil

1 onion, chopped

3 garlic cloves, chopped

3 jalapeño chiles, stemmed and chopped

1 cup chopped fresh *nopales* strips, Rajas (page 53) with ½ cup Crema (page 49), green beans, sweet corn, summer squash, peas, tender greens, asparagus, etc.

1 Tablespoon dried Mexican oregano

2 tomatoes, seeded, juiced, and chopped

½ teaspoon kosher salt

8 grinds of black pepper

8 eggs

12 warm flour or corn tortillas

1. Heat the oil to hot in a large skillet. Add the onion and sauté until transparent. Add the garlic, chiles, vegetable (or combination), and oregano. Cook, stirring, until the onion is golden and the vegetables still undercooked. Add the tomatoes, salt, and pepper and continue to cook for another minute.

2. Lightly whisk the eggs and add them to the skillet mixture. Scramble until the eggs are cooked to your liking. Pile onto plates and serve with warm tortillas.

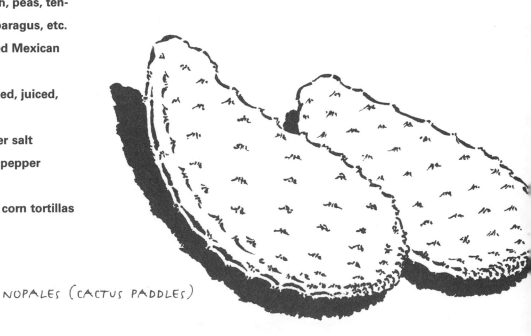

NOPALES (CACTUS PADDLES)

Ranch-Style Eggs
Huevos Rancheros

I've been making sojourns to Baja California since the early seventies, and one dish that has always been on Baja hotel restaurant menus is ranch-style eggs. It's a glorious late breakfast to enjoy on a bougainvillea-brightened patio. Tomato salsa is heated, then eggs are poached in the spicy red sauce. An order of huevos rancheros, Baja-style, means crisp tortillas slathered with refried beans, then topped with eggs and sauce. Additional warm tortillas or *bolillos* (chewy French rolls) are mandatory to dip into the yolks and beans. *Yield: 4 servings*

½ recipe Refried Beans
   (page 126)
½ cup vegetable oil
8 corn tortillas
½ recipe Basic Cooked Tomato
   Sauce (page 32)
8 eggs
1 avocado, peeled and sliced
1 lime, cut into wedges

1. Heat the refried beans.

2. In a skillet, heat the oil until you can see it ripple. Cook the tortillas, one at a time, until crisp. Drain on paper towels.

3. Bring the tomato sauce to a simmer and poach the eggs in the bubbling liquid (or you may fry the eggs in butter).

4. To assemble, place 2 tortillas on each of 4 plates. Smear about ¼ cup beans on each tortilla. Place an egg on each tortilla. Spoon sauce around (not over) the eggs. Arrange avocado slices and lime wedges on each plate.

Divorced Eggs
Huevos Divorciados

Restaurants around Morelia, Michoacán, serve this amusingly named dish because two tortillas and eggs are separated from each another by a barricade of refried beans. It's a good dish for leftover beans and sauces—and similar to *Huevos Rancheros* (page 151). A spoon of green tomatillo sauce is put on one tortilla, a spoon of red tomato sauce on the other, with a fried egg on top of each. Beans are arranged in a line between the two sections. Serve divorced beans with *bolillos,* chewy French rolls.

Yield: 2 servings

¼ cup vegetable oil

4 tortillas

1 cup Refried Beans (page 126)

½ cup Basic Cooked Tomato Sauce (page 32)

½ cup Basic Cooked Tomatillo Sauce (page 34)

1 Tablespoon butter

4 eggs

1. Heat the oil in a skillet. Fry the tortillas until they are crisp. Drain on paper towels. Discard the oil and wipe the skillet clean.

2. In a saucepan, reheat the leftover beans. In 2 more saucepans, reheat the sauces.

3. Heat butter in the cleaned skillet and fry the eggs to your liking.

4. On 2 oval plates, place 2 crisp tortillas on each, not touching one another. Put half the beans, in a line, in the center of each plate, separating the tortillas. Spoon red sauce on one tortilla, green sauce on the other, on both plates. Place a fried egg on each tortilla.

Spanish-Mexican Frittata
Tortilla Español

If you ever find yourself in Spain having a glass of sherry in a tapas bar, be sure to have a slice of classic potato and egg torte with your drink. Via Spain, *tortilla Español* has been popular in every Mexican colonial city for centuries and is enjoyed as an appetizer or light meal. It's not really an egg dish but a potato cake held together with eggs. This Mexican frittata is more flavorful than the dish prepared by Spanish ancestors thanks to browned potato pieces, caramelized onions, and fresh chiles. An uncooked table salsa is a perfect side touch. Because *tortilla Español* is best served warm or at room temperature, it makes a superb buffet dish.

Yield: 6 servings

3 Tablespoons olive oil

3 unpeeled red potatoes, diced into ¼-inch cubes

1 large onion, chopped

3 serrano or jalapeño chiles, stemmed and chopped

½ teaspoon cumin seed

6 eggs

2 Tablespoons dried Mexican oregano

¼ cup grated queso añejo or Parmesan cheese

1½ teaspoons kosher salt

8 grinds of black pepper

1. Heat 2 tablespoons of the oil in a wide skillet that can go under a broiler (nonstick or cast iron is best). Add the potatoes and stir to coat each piece with oil. Cook, without stirring, until the undersides are brown, then turn the cubes over. Brown the other sides. Remove cooked potatoes with a slotted spoon to paper towels and drain.

2. Heat another tablespoon of oil in the skillet, add the onion, and sauté until transparent. Add the chiles and cumin and cook until the onion is golden brown.

3. Break the eggs into a medium-size bowl and whisk lightly. Add the potatoes, onion mixture, oregano, cheese, salt, and pepper and mix gently.

4. Heat the skillet. Add the egg mixture to any oil remaining in the skillet and even the top. Turn down the heat and slowly simmer until the eggs are firm, about 15 minutes. Meanwhile, preheat the broiler. Remove the skillet from the heat and place it under the broiler for a minute for the top to set and lightly brown. Loosen the torte with a knife and slide it onto a serving plate. It slices best when not too hot.

Eggs Baked in Beans
Huevos con Frijoles al Horno

Eggs baked in beans is a super-simple, home-style meal when you have leftover beans. Enriqueta's children are deliriously happy when she prepares their favorite Jalisco dish. They love to scoop the egg and refried beans with crisp tortilla chips rather than using a fork. Serve with a big bowl of crunchy jícama spears squirted with fresh lime juice and sprinkled with chile powder (for a completely non-utensil-necessary meal).

Yield: 2 or 4 servings

4 cups refried or cooked and mashed beans without bean liquid (pink beans in Jalisco, but any type of beans may be used)

4 eggs

1 bag tortilla chips

1. Preheat the oven to 400°F.

2. In a greased 1-quart baking dish, spoon the beans in 4 mounds, with a well in the center of each.

3. Break an egg into each well. Bake for 12 minutes for medium-cooked eggs or as long as you prefer. With a large spoon, lift one portion of beans, including an egg, onto a plate and repeat with the others. Surround the egg with tortilla chips stuck into the beans for scooping.

Eggs and Cheese in Red Sauce
Salsa con Huevos y Queso

Susana Trilling, of Seasons of My Heart cooking school (page 213), shares this recipe from her friend Rosa. As Susana says, "It's great, simple, and delicious." What else could anyone want from a saucy Oaxacan dish? Eggs and cheese in red sauce is a family favorite from the cheese-making, tomato-growing area around Etla. It's a traditional mix of southern Mexican flavors never found in ersatz north-of-the-border joints. Put out a huge pile of warm corn tortillas and dig in.

Yield: 6 servings

4 pounds ripe plum tomatoes

2 or 3 fresh poblano or Anaheim chiles (Rosa uses the regional de agua chile of Oaxaca, which is *much* spicier)

2 Tablespoons vegetable oil

½ onion, chopped

1 teaspoon kosher salt

6 grinds of black pepper

1½ pounds ranchero or dry farmer cheese, cut into wedges

2 sprigs *epazote,* or 10 sprigs cilantro, tied

1 Tablespoon butter

12 eggs, lightly whisked in a bowl

1. Heat a *comal,* griddle, or heavy skillet. Toast (page 28) the tomatoes and chiles until their skins are black. Peel. Put in a blender and coarsely grind.

2. Heat the oil in a heavy pot. Add the onion and cook until golden. Add the blender ingredients and bring to a boil. Reduce the heat and cook at medium heat for 10 minutes. Taste and add the salt, less if the cheese is salty. Add the pepper. Reduce the heat to a simmer.

3. Add the cheese and *epazote* or cilantro.

4. Heat the butter in a skillet and pour in the eggs. Cook slowly until they form large clumps. Add to the sauce and gently stir together for a few seconds. Remove the *epazote* or cilantro and serve immediately with tortillas.

ISABELLA MORALES DE MÉNDEZ'S

Hard-Boiled Eggs Wrapped in Tortillas with Two Sauces
Papadzules

Everyone loves *papadzules*. These Yucatán treats are very simple to prepare, but look and taste as if they took all day. Corn tortillas are dipped in an easy-to-make *pipián* (pumpkin seed sauce), then rolled around hard-boiled egg quarters. (If you're a cholesterol watcher, egg whites only are delicious.) Tomato sauce is spooned around. *Cebolla Curtida* (recipe follows) is a mandatory accompaniment of vinegared mild red onions.

Yield: 8 papadzules (4 servings)

For the pumpkin seed sauce:

2 cups raw pumpkin seeds (green pepitas, found in health food stores)

½ teaspoon kosher salt

1 cup water

1. Toast (page 28) the pumpkin seeds and put in a blender container.

2. Add the salt and ½ cup of the water. Blend. Slowly add the remaining water and purée, adding additional water if necessary for a creamy sauce. Pour into a wide bowl.

For the papadzules:

8 corn tortillas

8 hard-boiled eggs, quartered

2 cups Basic Cooked Tomato Sauce (page 32), made with a few *epazote* sprigs, if possible

1. Heat 1 tortilla on both sides on a hot *comal* or in a heavy skillet. Put the tortilla in the pumpkin seed sauce and coat completely. Lay the tortilla on a plate.

2. Put a row of egg quarters on the tortilla, tip to tip, and roll it, seam side down. Continue with another *papadzul.* Cover with additional pumpkin seed sauce.

3. Spoon the tomato sauce around the *papadzules.* Continue with the other 3 portions. Top with *Cebolla Curtida* (recipe follows).

1 large red onion

½ cup white vinegar

½ teaspoon salt

1 habanero chile (optional)

Cebolla Curtida

1. Cut the onion into ¼-inch slices. Break up the slices into rings and put in a strainer. Wash with cold water to make sure the onions are mild, then dry.

2. Put the onions in a bowl and mix with the vinegar and salt. If you like heat, toast the habanero chile and nestle it, whole, in the onions. It will flavor and add spice to the entire bowl of onions, but keep a fire extinguisher handy for anyone who takes a bite.

EPAZOTE

Desserts and Sweets

MEXICO'S FAVORITE DESSERT IS A SIMPLE SELECTION OF ITS unparalleled tropical fruit, peeled and beautifully presented—and sprinkled with fresh lime juice or Mexican dark rum. Flan is on every home and serious restaurant table—the creamy version here is sublime; *Cajeta,* goat milk caramel, fills elegant crepes and tops coffee ice cream; and hot Mexican chocolate sauce slithers over vanilla bean ice cream. Have some fun with a few contemporary recipes such as a chocolate custard bread pudding; Outrageous Mole Brownies are as delightful as Avocado Popsicles.

Creamy Baked Flan
Flan

Unlike the dense flans in *A Cook's Tour of Mexico* that are cut with a knife and eaten with a fork, Estela's flan is so light and creamy that you have to scoop it out of its baking dish with a long-handled spoon. Estela makes her easy, custardy flan with two different weight creams in her mountain home on the outskirts of Toluca. Fabulous dairy products are a staple there. Half-and-half works perfectly well in the U.S. Serve cold.

Yield: 12 servings

¾ cup sugar

3 Tablespoons water

7 eggs

½ cup sugar

1 rounded teaspoon ground *canela,* or 1 scant teaspoon ground cinnamon

1 teaspoon pure vanilla extract

¼ teaspoon kosher salt

1 quart half-and-half

1. Preheat the oven to 350°F.

2. Put the ¾ cup sugar and water in a small heavy saucepan. Heat on high. Swirl the pan to dissolve the sugar. When the liquid is caramel-colored, pour it into the bottom of a 2-quart ceramic soufflé dish or similar deep casserole.

3. With a mixer or whisk, beat the eggs and ½ cup sugar in a large bowl. Sprinkle the *canela* over the mixture and whisk again. Whisk in the vanilla and salt.

4. Scald (heat until tiny bubbles form around the sides of a saucepan) the half-and-half. Pour it, in a slow ribbon, into the egg mixture, whisking. Pour the mixture into the soufflé dish. Set the dish in a large baking pan. Pour hot water into the outer baking pan until the water reaches about 1 inch up the sides of the baking dish.

5. Bake for 35 minutes. When lumps adhere to the side of a small knife, remove the dish from the oven and from the water bath. Cool at room temperature, then refrigerate until chilled. Be sure to reach down and get some caramel for each serving.

INEZ MARTINEZ DE GALINDO'S

Creamy Rice Pudding
Arroz con Leche

What could be a better finale to a meal spiked with spicy chiles? Vanilla, orange, and *canela* perfume the creamy rice pudding that's best served cool or at room temperature—optimum temperatures after hot salsas. A tiny scoop of ice cream or whipped cream turns the dessert into party fare. If you live in the South, garnish each serving with fresh orange leaves from your tree, as Inez does at her home near Taxco. Besides its stunning beauty, Taxco's claim to fame is myriad silver ateliers and shops offering the country's finest silver table settings and serving pieces.

Yield: 6 servings

½ cup medium- or long-grain white rice

3 cups milk, either whole or low fat

½ teaspoon pure vanilla extract

Pinch of kosher salt

2 three-inch *canela* sticks, or ½ teaspoon ground cinnamon

1 teaspoon finely minced orange zest

½ cup *piloncillo (panela)* or dark brown sugar

Cooking spray or butter to grease the casserole dish

1. Preheat the oven to 325°F.

2. In a saucepan, combine the rice and 1 quart water. Bring to a boil and boil for 5 minutes. Drain the rice.

3. Meanwhile, combine the milk, vanilla, salt, *canela*, and zest in another saucepan. Bring to a boil, watching carefully so the milk does not boil over. Remove from the heat and add the *piloncillo*.

4. Stir the rice into the milk mixture. Pour into a 3-quart, deep, greased casserole (including the *canela* stick, if using, but try not to break it up). Bake, covered, without stirring, for 1 hour, until most, but not all, of the liquid is absorbed. Remove the *canela* before serving.

Three-Milk Cake
Pastel Tres Leches

Ladies who take tea in the afternoon and children all over Mexico adore this traditional ring-shaped cake. Reyna's (see page 213) two grown sons actually offer to help in the kitchen when she's making their favorite dessert. Nowadays, nonstick Bundt pans make unmolding a cinch, and because the rich, moist cake is made a day ahead and refrigerated, try this Mexican favorite for a party when a make-ahead dessert is welcome.

Yield: 8 servings

6 eggs, separated

½ cup sugar

1 cup sifted flour

1 can (14 ounces) sweetened condensed milk

1 can (12 fluid ounces) evaporated milk

1 cup heavy whipping cream

3 Tablespoons brandy or orange liqueur

1 teaspoon pure vanilla extract

1. Preheat the oven to 400°F.

2. Grease a Bundt pan (preferably nonstick) and/or spray twice with cooking oil.

3. Beat the egg whites with ¼ cup of the sugar until they hold stiff peaks. Beat the egg yolks with the remaining ¼ cup sugar until they reach a thick, custardlike texture. Combine the egg whites and yolks. Sprinkle the flour over the mixture and delicately fold everything together, keeping as much air in the eggs as possible. Do not overmix.

4. Pour the mixture into the Bundt pan and delicately run a spatula over it so the top is somewhat even in the pan. Put the cake in the oven and immediately turn down the heat to 300°F. Bake for 25 minutes, just until it's beginning to turn pale golden. Remove from the oven and let cool for at least 15 minutes at room temperature. Reyna unmolds the cake (it will have collapsed in the pan) then immediately returns it to the Bundt pan. This step ensures easy removal later.

5. Mix the condensed milk with the evaporated milk, cream, brandy, and vanilla. Pour the mixture over the cake while it is still in the Bundt pan. Let soak, refrigerated, for 12 hours; it may be kept in the refrigerator for up to 2 days. Unmold the cake onto a plate with a lip to catch any sauce.

Mexican Chocolate Sauce
Salsa de Chocolate Mexicana

Mexican chocolate is a different animal than the bittersweet or milk chocolate we're used to: It's not for eating. Mexican chocolate is always served hot, melted with water or milk to make a cup of hot chocolate. Oaxaca's superb chocolate is a combination of Mexican *cacao* beans, sugar, almonds, and *canela* (true Ceylon cinnamon). If you're using lesser-quality Abuelta or Ibarra brands common in the U.S., add more *canela* or cinnamon to taste. Add pulverized almonds if you like, though it's unnecessary. After the cream is added and everything melts, this sauce will be your new best friend. Pour a generous portion over a bowl of vanilla-bean ice cream topped with toasted almond pieces for the perfect dessert after a spicy dinner. Leftovers (sure!) can be refrigerated.

Yield: about 2 cups

8 ounces Mexican chocolate
 tablets or bittersweet
 chocolate

½ teaspoon ground *canela* or ¼
 teaspoon ground cinnamon

1 Tablespoon butter

1 teaspoon pure vanilla extract

Small pinch of salt

1 cup heavy whipping cream

1. In a double boiler, melt the chocolate, *canela,* and butter.
2. Add the vanilla and salt. Slowly add the cream, stirring with a small whisk until smooth. Serve warm.

Crepes with Caramel Sauce and Toasted Nuts
Crepas con Cajeta

Crepes have been popular in Mexico since generations past when the country was ruled by France. Ferdinand Maximillian, a Hapsburg, Austria archduke, was sent by Napoleon III to rule as emperor of Mexico. His tenure was cut short (1864-1867) when Maximillian was shot by Benito Juárez's firing squad.

Cajeta is a sweet goat's milk caramel beloved throughout Mexico, especially near Celaya, home to the luscious sauce. The caramel is a perfect complement to crepes with toasted pecans (or walnuts). A scoop of vanilla-bean or coffee ice cream only enhances the experience.

Yield: 4 servings

For traditional cajeta, *2½ hours:*
Yield: 2 cups (enough for leftovers)

1 quart goat's milk, available in health food stores (if you can't find it, *dulce de leche*, adored by Argentinians, is the exact same sauce made with cow's milk, so use cow's milk instead, for a different flavor)
2 cups sugar

1. Combine the milk and sugar in a heavy nonstick saucepan. Heat, over high heat, stirring with a wooden spoon, for about 10 minutes, until the milk begins to simmer.

2. Reduce the heat and keep at a constant simmer until the mixture is a light caramel color, stirring every 5 minutes or so for 2 hours. The sauce will be reduced by half.

3. Stir constantly for the last 10 minutes as the mixture foams and thickens to a caramel sauce consistency and the color becomes golden tan. The sauce thickens as it cools.

Note: For quick *cajeta,* boil a can of sweetened condensed goat's milk until it has reduced, thickened, and turned caramel-colored.

For the crepes:

Yield: 8 5-inch dessert crepes

1 egg

¼ cup water

⅓ cup milk

1½ Tablespoons vegetable oil, plus ½ teaspoon for the pan

2 Tablespoons sugar

Pinch of salt

½ cup flour

7 wax paper squares cut slightly larger than the crepes

1. Beat the egg in a bowl. Add the water, milk, and oil and stir. Gradually stir in the sugar, salt, and flour. Let the batter rest for 15 minutes before using.

2. Heat a nonstick small skillet (about 6 inches wide at the bottom) to hot and brush it lightly with oil. A drop of water should spit and spatter.

3. Spoon 2 tablespoons batter in the pan and immediately start rotating it by the handle so that the batter is evenly distributed over the pan bottom. Bubbles will form over the surface. Cook for 30 seconds. With help from a spatula, if necessary, turn the crepe over to lightly brown the other side, 15 to 20 seconds more (this splotchy side will be the inside of the folded crepe). Begin stacking the crepes on a plate with a sheet of wax paper between.

For the nuts:

⅓ cup chopped pecans or walnuts

1. Heat a *comal* or skillet to hot.

2. Add the nuts and toast, turning constantly so they don't burn. When their color changes to light brown, immediately remove from the hot *comal* to a small bowl.

To assemble:

1. Put a warm crepe on a plate, splotchy side up. Spread 2 or 3 tablespoons warm *cajeta* over the crepe. Fold in half then in half again to form a triangle. Put on a serving plate and repeat. Each serving contains 2 crepes.

2. Scatter toasted nuts over the crepes and serve warm.

(Continued)

Variations:

Coffee Ice Cream with *Cajeta* and Toasted Nuts
For an easy dessert, you can buy jars of *cajeta* in most U.S. Latino stores (a time saver for *cajeta* crepes as well). Purchase good-quality coffee ice cream and top with warmed *cajeta*. Sprinkle with toasted nuts.

Poached Pears with *Cajeta*
Gently simmer 6 peeled, halved, and cored pears in 2 cups red or white wine, 2 cups water, 1½ cups sugar, and 2 three-inch *canela* sticks for about 12 minutes. Cool in the liquid for 30 minutes. Place 2 pear halves on each plate and top with *cajeta* and a sprinkle of toasted nuts.

Broiled Pineapple with Rum Sauce
Piña con Panela y Ron

La Laguna, just south of Veracruz City, is home to miles of pineapple plantations—all with gorgeous Gulf views. From these pineapples, locals devise all sorts of concoctions, from vinegars to salsas to rum-spiked drinks and desserts. This pineapple dessert was a Sunday special at Irma's open-sided, thatched-roof restaurant in nearby Boca del Rio. A small scoop of pineapple sherbet on top is both traditional and something close to paradise. *Yield: 4 servings*

¾ cup *piloncillo (panela)* or
    dark brown sugar

1 Tablespoon water

1 Tablespoon dark rum

1 Tablespoon butter

⅓ cup chopped pecans or
    walnuts

1 large ripe pineapple

Vanilla ice cream

1. Heat the grill to hot.

2. In a small heavy saucepan, heat the *piloncillo* and water until the sugar melts, swirling the pan to form a syrupy caramel. Remove the pan from the heat and carefully drizzle the rum down the pan sides because the caramel may bubble and splatter. Return to the heat and simmer, stirring in the butter. The sauce may be made 2 days ahead and chilled. Reheat before serving warm.

3. Toast the nuts on a *comal* or in a small, ungreased skillet until they are lightly browned.

4. Slice across the pineapple 1 inch below the leaves and ½ inch above the base. Cut off the rind and any brown "eyes" that are attached to the fruit. Cut the pineapple into 8 slices about ½ inch thick. If necessary, cut the slices in half and trim away any hard center areas.

5. Place the slices on a very hot grill and grill just long enough so grill marks show on the fruit. Turn over and cook the other side. Place 2 slices on each dessert plate. Spoon warm rum sauce over the pineapple slices and sprinkle with toasted nuts.

DOÑA ESPERANZA DE SEPÚLVEDA'S

Fruit Dessert Made with Quince
Ate de Membrillo

Esperancita (an endearing nickname for Esperanza) is very proud of her pale golden quince-paste dessert. One afternoon as we sat in her kitchen, she shared a plate of gorgeously gold *ate* given to her by a friend, but couldn't help commenting, "Mine is paler—really light yellow—the best." The Pátzcuaro grandmother says her *ate* is lighter than just about any of her friends', and certainly lighter than commercial varieties, because she doesn't cook the fruit in hot sugar syrup, which, she claims, turns the paste dark. Esperancita also rubs the fruit through plastic (nonmetal) screening attached to a home-made wood frame, and she cooks her paste in a nonreactive enamel pot. Prepare *ate* at least 2 days in advance of serving because the natural fruit pectins need time to set and harden, and the flavor becomes more intense. Cut the *ate* in slices about ½ inch thick. Serve *ate* with slices of Mexican panela cheese, cream cheese, or other white, mild cheese. Some people also enjoy not-too-sweet cookies alongside.

Yield: 8 servings

2 pounds quinces

2 pounds sugar

2 cups water

1. Scrub the quinces very well. Quarter and put them in a pot of boiling water. Esperancita says, "when the quinces open like a flower and the texture becomes spongy" (about 30 minutes), drain well. Peel and remove the cores.

2. Rub the fruit pulp through a plastic-screened strainer, or make a strainer like Esperancita's with plastic screening staple-gunned to a wooden frame. This is work, but, with the back of a large wooden spoon, push all the paste through the screen into a large nonreactive pot. Nontraditionalists can use a food processor with the plastic blade.

3. Heat the paste with the sugar and water in a deep heavy pot over high heat. Cook, stirring to dissolve the sugar. When you pull up the spoon and the thick paste no longer falls off (about 2 hours), rapidly pour the hot paste into a deep plate with a lip, to harden. It should be about 1 inch

168   MEATLESS MEXICAN HOME COOKING

thick. Because quince (and guava) has huge amounts of natural pectin, the *ate* will begin to set immediately. *Ate* is best if you cover it with plastic wraping and refrigerate for 2, or better yet 3, days before slicing.

Variation:

Guava *Ate*

Put 2 pounds (4 cups) guava (any type or color guava) pulp in a pot with 2 cups water. Bring to a full, rolling boil, then reduce the heat and simmer for 30 minutes, uncovered. Remove from the heat and cool for about 15 minutes. Purée in a processor or blender; there will be about 3 cups purée. Return to the pot, add 2 cups sugar, and stir in 2 tablespoons lime juice. Follow step 3 above.

GUAVAS

Mexican Bread Dessert
Capriotada

apriotada is probably not exactly what Buckminster Fuller had in mind when he coined the term *synergy,* but here's a fine example of the whole being greater than its parts. Thrifty Mexican cooks easily toss together this leftover-laden dessert. Lupita's recipe is from the state of Veracruz, but *capriotada* can be found in any Mexican kitchen where a scrap of bread is never thrown away. Some frugal cooks fry stale bread in oil to add richness; others pour melted butter over bread layered with cream cheese; some deep-fry egg-battered bread slices for a French toast effect; yet others brush stale bread with butter and an egg wash before layering in the casserole. This less rich version cuts calories but not flavor.

Yield: 8 servings

1 pound stale *pan de yema* (Mexican egg bread), or Jewish challah, or brioche, or French bread, cut into 1-inch pieces

1 cup coarsly chopped pecans or walnuts

6 stale corn tortillas

3 cups *piloncillo (panela)* or dark brown sugar

2 four-inch *canela* sticks, or 1 four-inch cinnamon stick, or 1 teaspoon ground cinnamon

3 Tablespoons butter

4 cups water

2 cups apple juice

1 cup raisins, or other dried fruit, chopped

1. Heat the oven to 325°F. Spread the bread cubes in one layer on a baking sheet. Completely dry the bread but do not let it brown, turning it once or twice, for about 12 minutes. Meanwhile, on another baking sheet, lightly toast the nuts in the oven.

2. Grease a deep, 2-quart casserole dish. Line it with overlapping tortillas.

3. Put the *piloncillo, canela,* butter, water, and apple juice in a saucepan and bring to a boil. Reduce the heat and simmer for about 20 minutes, until the liquid is a light syrup.

4. Mix the bread, nuts, raisins, and cheese in a large bowl. Pour the syrup through a strainer (not necessary if ground cinnamon is used) over the bread mixture and stir gently. Let the bread absorb the liquid for 10 minutes.

5. Bake for 30 minutes. Sprinkle with granulated sugar and continue to bake until the top is golden and the texture firm. Scoop onto plates, leaving the tortillas—they are generally not eaten.

1½ cups crumbled queso fresco, or dry farmer cheese, or dry cottage cheese, or a combination

¼ cup granulated sugar

Variation: *Capriotada* is a typical meatless Lenten main course dish throughout Mexico—the addition of vegetables and additional cheese makes it so. Add 1 thinly sliced onion, 3 thickly sliced tomatoes, 1 teaspoon salt, 8 grinds of black pepper, and 1 cup shredded mild melting cheese such as quesillo de Oaxaca, mozzarella, or Monterey Jack and some queso añejo or Parmesan sprinkled on top.

CANELA (TRUE CEYLON CINNAMON)

MARCELA LÓPEZ BRUN'S

Mexican Chocolate Custard Bread Pudding
Postre con Pan y Chocolate

Bread pudding is Mexico's favorite home-style dessert. At Marcela's house in Puebla, the old standby, *Capriotada* (page 170), is updated with a non-Mexican custard base and enhanced with Oaxaca's fabulous almond- and *canela*-flavored chocolate. In the U.S., substitute Mexican Iberra or Abulita brands, or bittersweet. Serve this rich dessert warm, with a scoop of real vanilla-bean ice cream to melt alongside.

Yield: 6 servings

½ **pound stale** *pan de yema*
   (Mexican egg bread), or
   Jewish challah, or brioche,
   or French bread, torn into
   2-inch pieces
¼ **pound butter, melted**
2 **cups milk**
2 **four-inch** *canela* **sticks, or 1**
   four-inch cinnamon stick
6 **ounces Mexican or bitter-**
   sweet chocolate, broken into
   small pieces
3 **eggs**
Pinch of salt
½ **cup** *piloncillo (panela)* **or**
   dark brown sugar
1 **cup slivered almonds,**
   toasted
1 **Golden Delicious apple,**
   peeled and chopped

1. Heat the oven to 325°F. Spread the bread in one layer on a baking sheet. Drizzle with the melted butter. Completely dry the bread but do not let it brown, turning it once or twice, for about 15 minutes.

2. In a saucepan over medium heat, bring the milk to a simmer with the *canela*. Remove from the heat and add the chocolate, stirring until it melts into the milk.

3. In a large bowl, beat the eggs with the salt and *piloncillo*. Add the nuts and apple. Stir in the milk mixture and bread. Let this mixture stand for 10 minutes to allow the bread to absorb the liquid. Pick out as much of the *canela* as possible.

4. Butter a deep 2-quart casserole dish and spoon in the bread mixture. Press down on the mixture—it should be 2 to 3 inches thick with no air pockets and the surface evenly flat. Cover the casserole dish with foil poked with a few air holes to let steam escape. Bake in the center of the oven for 40 minutes, remove the foil, and bake for 10 minutes, or until the mixture feels firm and the top looks glossy.

Cinnamon-Sugared and Fried Pastries
Buñuelos

Buñuelos are considered fiesta food by most Mexicans and are eaten during celebrations. In Oaxaca an enchanting food tradition takes place outside the cathedral during fiesta days, especially around Christmas. The crisp pastries are broken up and placed in ceramic bowls, then splashed with sugar syrup. After celebrants eat their *buñuelos* they make a wish and smash the bowl on the cathedral grounds. Because there's always a line in front of the *buñuelo* vendor, it leads one to think the good luck system works.

A contemporary way to serve *buñuelos* is to mold the flat disks into a bowl shape while they're still hot. Rather than moistening with a sugar syrup made from *piloncillo*, cinnamon, and water, top the crunchy cookie bowl with a scoop of ice cream.

Yield: 12 buñuelos

3 cups flour, plus extra

1 teaspoon baking powder

¼ teaspoon salt

1 Tablespoon sugar

4 Tablespoons butter or
    vegetable shortening, melted

2 eggs

½ cup milk

Oil for deep frying

½ cup sugar

1 teaspoon ground cinnamon

1. Mix 3 cups flour with the baking powder, salt, and 1 tablespoon sugar.

2. In another bowl, whisk the butter, eggs, and milk. Slowly add the flour mixture and combine to form a dough. Sprinkle additional flour over the dough and mix until a smooth, elastic dough is formed.

3. Cut the dough into 12 pieces and form into balls. Put the balls on a dish, cover tightly with plastic wrap, and refrigerate 30 minutes.

4. On a floured surface roll the balls into thin disks using a rolling pin dusted with flour. The disks should be about 12 inches in diameter.

5. Heat the oil to 375°F. Fry one *buñuelo* at a time until crisp. Drain on paper towels.

6. Combine the sugar and cinnamon and sprinkle the still-warm buñuelos with the mixture.

Chocolate-Chile Mole Brownies

If you're a lover of moist, chewy, bittersweet chocolate brownies, here's my sensational new Mexican twist on the old U.S.A. favorite. Ancho chile's smoky-sweet fruit and slight anise flavor (yet not spicy) complements dark chocolate perfectly. Generations of Mexican *mole*-makers can testify to that.

Yield: 2 dozen 2-inch brownies

4 ounces unsweetened
   chocolate

¼ pound butter

2 large eggs (use 3 eggs if a
   cakelike texture is preferred)

2 cups sugar

1 teaspoon pure vanilla extract

2 teaspoons pulverized *canela,*
   or 1 teaspoon ground
   cinnamon

3 Tablespoons ancho chile
   powder (or pulverize 3
   stemmed, seeded, and
   toasted ancho chiles)

1 cup flour

¼ cup toasted sesame seeds

1 cup chopped walnuts

1. Preheat oven to 350°F. Butter an 8 x 12-inch baking dish (or use nonstick cooking spray).

2. Melt the chocolate with the butter in the top of a double boiler. Remove from the heat to cool.

3. With an electric mixer, beat the eggs, sugar, vanilla, *canela,* and chile powder. Stir the chocolate into the egg mixture, then stir in the flour, sesame seeds, and walnuts. The dough will be sticky.

4. Turn the mixture into the prepared pan and spread it evenly. Bake for 22 to 23 minutes, or until the center is just set. Do not overbake or the brownies will lose their chewy texture and the edges will be overdone. Cool in the pan for at least 30 minutes before cutting into squares.

Variations: Substitute chopped almonds or pecans for the walnuts. In place of ancho chile, try pasilla or guajillo chile—do not use chile that is very spicy. Add ½ cup bittersweet chocolate chips.

Avocado Popsicles
Paletas de Aguacate

Could any sweet treat be more simple or satisfying after spicy salsa than an avocado popsicle? These fun-time goodies are a big kid's delight, so make them for a grown-up dessert. Marilyn (page 212) offers avocado popsicles to legions of fans while she guides them on folk art expeditions around her home base of Lake Pátzcuaro, Michoacán. The region is also known as Mexico's avocado capital.

Yield: 6 popsicles

2 large, ripe Hass (formerly known as Haas) avocados, about 2 pounds

½ cup granulated sugar

1 cup heavy cream

2 Tablespoons fresh lime juice

6 flat popsicle sticks or teaspoons

2 plastic popsicle trays (3 popsicles each) or 6 paper cups

1. Cut the avocados in half and remove the pits. Scoop the flesh into a blender or processor container. Purée until completely smooth.

2. In a saucepan over medium heat, stir the sugar and cream just until the sugar dissolves. Pour into the avocado purée with the lime juice and mix.

3. Place the blender container in the refrigerator to chill. Freeze in an ice cream freezer according to the manufacturer's directions. Fill the popsicle trays or paper cups. When partially set, insert sticks. Freeze until firm.

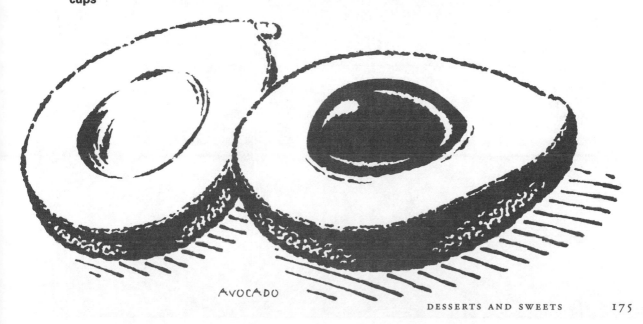

AVOCADO

Drinks

MEXICO'S HOT, HUMID COASTAL CLIMATE AND HIGH-ALTITUDE, bone-dry inland air bring about mega thirsts. Add serious sunbathing, archeological site exploring, plus passionate shopping and your throat's the Mohave. Thank goodness Mexico has some of the world's wettest quenchers, from margaritas and sangrítas to beers, blended fruit drinks, and homegrown coffee. *Aguas Frescas* are classic market drinks brewed from rice, hibiscus flowers, citrus, tamarind pods, or chia seeds, among other standbys popular long before bottled sodas stole the show.

Mezcalitos and Tequila Shooters
Bebidas de Mezcal y Tequila

Both mezcal and tequila are made from the succulent *agave,* called *maguey* in Spanish. To produce booze, the plant's heart is cut out with a machete (visions of Aztec warriors here) and the blood—oops, liquid—is extracted. Heat extracts the sugar and fermentation begins for distillation. Mezcal continues to be mainly a Oaxacan backyard brew made from various species of agave, but a few brands are distilled in contemporary stainless steel tanks. Tequila, on the other hand, is government-controlled; it's made from only one type of agave, *Agave tequilana,* Weber blue variety; and it can be grown only in five government-specified Mexican states—the best is from Jalisco. Many Mexicans enjoy mezcal as apéritifs-digestifs; 100 percent agave tequilas are in a class by themselves. Some aged tequilas are regarded with the same esteem as fine aged Cognacs and are drunk from snifters.

Yield: 2 drinks each, tequila and mezcal

For Mezcalitos:

2 *copitas,* tiny earthenware cups that hold about 2 ounces

A bottle of quality mezcal, such as Oro de Oaxaca

1. Pour mezcal almost to the brim of each cup.

2. Toast by clinking *copitas* and saying, *¡Salud!* Sip. Repeat.

Variation: *Mezcalitos* with Salt, Lime and *Gusanos*

1. Rub the rims of 2 *copitas* with a lime wedge and dip in *gusano*-flavored salt (*gusanos* are the grubs in some mezcal bottles), or mix kosher salt with spicy chile powder.

2. Fill with mezcal. Sip as an apéritif.

For Tequila Shooters:

2 Mexican glasses that are tall, thin shot glasses and hold about 2 ounces liquid

A bottle of 100-percent agave tequila *reposado* (aged in oak at least 2 months) or tequila *añejo* (aged longer)

1. Pour tequila almost to the brim of each glass.

2. Toast. Sip. Repeat.

Variation: Tequila Shooters with Salt and Lime

1. Put a pinch of coarse or kosher salt in the fleshy area on your hand between your thumb and index finger. Lick.

2. Bite into a wedge of lime and quickly suck the juice.

3. Shoot back a glass of tequila. Repeat. Repeat. Try to walk.

World's Best Margarita
Tequila, Cointreau, and Lime Drink

Bo-Bo, a Guadalajara bartender, shared his quintessential margarita when I was writing *A Cook's Tour of Mexico*. Since the book's publication, more people have declared their unabashed love for this recipe than I can count. And no wonder—it's phenomenal—and it turns any quiet get-together into a fiesta. The simplest, finest ingredients poured over ice cubes, rather than whirled into sugary slush, make one mean margarita.

Yield: 1 drink

Lime wedges

2 Tablespoons kosher salt or
    coarse sea salt

Ice cubes

1½ parts 100-percent agave
    tequila, either silver (clear) or
    reposado (aged for a few
    months in oak), to be
    decadent

¼ part Cointreau

1 part freshly squeezed lime
    juice, if possible from Key
    limes

1. Rub a glass (about 4 inches high and 3 inches wide) with a lime wedge, then dip the rim in coarse salt, not finely textured table salt. Add ice cubes.

2. Mix the tequila, Cointreau, and lime juice in a pitcher. Carefully pour the mixture into the glass without messing the salted rim. Place a slice of lime on the rim. *¡Salud!*

Note: Limes in the U.S. (other than Key limes) are more sour, and generally less juicy, than Mexican limes, which are the same variety as Key limes. A margarita's sour first sip is important, but many people feel a little additional Cointreau or granulated sugar is necessary when using U.S. limes. Taste, then judge.

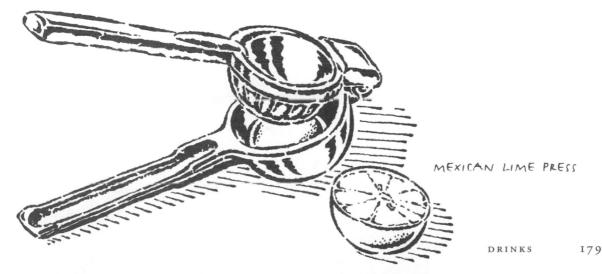

MEXICAN LIME PRESS

Spicy Citrus Juice and Tequila Drink
Sangríta

The first time I saw this drink, Carmen Ramirez Degollado, owner of Mexico City's El Bajio restaurant (page 211), was sipping a two-fisted cocktail that caught my attention. One tiny glass held a red liquid, and a matching glass was filled to the brim with amber tequila. She offered me a sip (or, I should say, two sips)—first tequila and then the sangríta chaser—and I've been hooked ever since.

Sangríta (not to be confused with *sangría)* is a slightly sweet, spicy juice blend drunk alongside tequila. The blend is made with orange juice, tomato juice, and hot sauce. For four people you'll need eight tiny Mexican sangríta glasses. Sangríta glasses are taller and thinner than the typical shot glasses you see bartenders using. Often they are made of hand-blown thick glass and the rim is colored blue. Others are simple clear glasses. Try to find the real thing because the glasses make a difference—trust me. Dip four glasses in salt, then fill with the juice blend. Fill the other four glasses with 100-percent agave tequila. Sip from the tequila first, then the sangríta chaser, and keep on going.

Yield: about 2 cups, 8 servings

1 cup orange juice, cold

1 cup tomato juice, cold

½ teaspoon Tabasco or similar hot sauce, or more to taste

1 lime, quartered

3 Tablespoons kosher salt

100-percent agave tequila, preferably *reposado* or *anejo* that's been aged in oak

1. In a small pitcher, mix the juices and hot sauce.

2. Spread the kosher salt in a saucer. Run a wedge of lime around the rim of 4 glasses, then dip the rims in the coarsely textured salt.

3. Carefully pour sangríta into each glass with a salt rim. Fill the remaining salt-free glasses with tequila.

Limeade, Tequila, and Wine Drink
Sangría Preparada

Sangría preparada is always made in tall, clear glasses to show off its attractive presentation. The drink naturally separates into two layers: red wine floats above limeade that's been enhanced with a shot of clear tequila or vodka.

I can't help but remember the evening in a San Miguel de Allende patio restaurant when my husband, Morris, and I had just toasted with *sangrías preparadas*. In strolls a young French woman looking lost to the world and in need of somewhere to sit. We invited her over, shared our dinner, and asked about her plans in town. She was looking for porn shows. Surprised, to say the least, especially in Catholic San Miguel, we asked if maybe she didn't have the wrong town. Not until she described, in her strong French accent, their quality wools and rich colors, did we realize she was searching for ponchos.

Yield: 6 drinks

1 cup freshly squeezed lime juice (from Key, or Mexican limes if possible)

⅔ cup sugar

4 cups water

1 cup clear (silver), 100-percent agave tequila or vodka

1 cup dry red wine such as a young Zinfandel

1. Mix the lime juice and sugar in a pitcher until the sugar is dissolved. Add the water and tequila. Stir. Taste, and add additional sugar if the limes are very sour.

2. Fill 6 tall glasses with ice cubes. Add an equal amount of the limeade to each.

3. Tilt a glass and slowly pour in wine to form a separate layer over the limeade bottom layer. Serve with a brightly colored plastic straw (for stirring) and a slice of chartreuse green lime on the glass rim.

MEXICAN LIME WEDGES

Jamaica Flower Drink, and Jamaica Sangría

Agua de Jamaica, y Sangría de Jamaica

Jamaica is the dried-flower covering of a hibiscus family plant. When it's steeped in sweetened water it becomes one of Mexico's most popular traditional drinks and is ideal on those hot summer evenings when only a refreshing, slightly sour (similar to cranberry) drink will do. *(Jamaica* is the ruby *agua fresca* in the lineup of alcohol-free, psychedelic-colored liquids in large jars seen in markets all over Mexico.) *Jamaica* sangría, with alcohol added, is a New Year's tradition in Mexico. Its intense red is best shown off in an ice-filled glass punch bowl.

Yield: about 12 servings

For jamaica *drink:*

2 cups *jamaica* **flowers, found in Latino markets**

1½ cups sugar

6 cups water

1. Rinse the dried *jamaica* flowers. Place the flowers and sugar in a pot with the water and bring to a boil. Remove from the heat and let the liquid steep at room temperature for at least 3 hours.

2. Strain the liquid into a bowl using a paper coffee filter over a strainer. Press down on the flowers to extract all their color and discard the flowers. Taste, and add additional sugar if it's too tart, or more water if too strong (do not add more water if making sangría). *Jamaica* keeps, covered and refrigerated, up to 5 days.

For jamaica *sangría:*

1 bottle (750 ml) chilled dry, young, red wine

2 cups orange juice, chilled

1 bag ice cubes

1 orange, sliced

3 limes, sliced

1. Pour the *jamaica* drink (above) into a punch bowl. Stir in the wine and orange juice. Empty a bag of ice into the bowl. Top with orange slices.

2. Place a slice of lime on the rim of each glass.

Variation: For a quick party drink, add 1 jigger clear (silver) 100-percent agave tequila or vodka to a glass of *jamaica*.

CARMEN RAMÍREZ DEGOLLADO'S

Limeade with Chía Seed
Limonada con Chía

With huge piles of tiny Key limes elbowing out other fruits in many Mexican markets, is it any wonder limes are turned into limeade with such a furor? And what could be a more welcome drink with all the dishes that crave a squirt of lime? The special ingredients in this cooler are chía seeds. Their notoriety is that they're the seeds that, when watered, become the green "fur" on those odd terracotta animals known as Chía Pets. Chía is in the sage family and the seeds have a mild, citrus flavor and turn gelatinous when wet. They are found in Latino markets and many health food stores. Chía's strange texture and bizarre charcoal color make this limeade unusual, to say the least, but it will soon become one of your favorite refreshers. To taste it perfectly made, sample a pitcher at El Bajío restaurant in Mexico City (page 211)—you'll need it with owner Carmen's spicy chipotle chile salsa. *Yield: 5 cups*

1 quart water

1 cup fresh lime juice

½ cup sugar (plus extra if desired)

2 Tablespoons chía seeds

1. Pour the water into a large pitcher. Add the lime juice, sugar, and chía seeds.

2. Let the seeds plump and change texture until they become gelatinous, about 1 hour. Stir well and taste. Add additional sugar if desired. Refrigerate. The seeds sink to the pitcher bottom. Stir, pour over ice, and serve immediately.

Blended Mango Drink
Liquado de Mango

When you're traveling to Mexico and have roamed through an open-air market all morning and your feet begin to drag, your sinuses have maxed-out inhaling chile fumes, and your throat is so parched you can't speak anymore, head over to the nearest juice counter, pull up a stool, and order this combination *pronto*. Or make it yourself at home on a warm day—it couldn't be simpler. Other ripe fruits such as peaches, plums, pineapples, papayas, bananas, melons, and strawberries are ravishing alternatives to mangoes. Feel free to mix and match and to substitute orange juice for the water. The general drink ratio is 1 cup *very* ripe fruit to 1 cup water, 1 tablespoon sugar, and a squirt of lime juice.
Yield: 1 drink

1 cup ripe mango chunks

1 cup cold water

½ to 1 lime, juiced

1 Tablespoon sugar

1. Put the mango pieces, water, lime juice, and sugar in a blender container and blend at high speed until foamy.

2. Pour the golden liquid through a strainer into a tall glass and serve with a brightly colored plastic straw.

MANGOES

Cold Rice Drink
Horchata

Horchata is one of the few drinks that can actually relieve the shock caused by a mouthful of habanero chile. Think of the opaque, milky white refresher as liquefied rice pudding. It's similar in concept to how an Indian *lassi* complements spicy curries. Instant, dilutable *horchata* is sold in bottles, but nothing comes close to this authentic classic. The cold and creamy rice libation is found in traditional food markets throughout Mexico. My favorite is offered at Casilda's in the Juárez market in Oaxaca, where you can order it with a dab of raspberry-colored pureéd *tuna* (prickly pear cactus fruit) and chopped nuts.
Yield: about 2 quarts

1 cup medium- or long-grain
   white rice
9 cups water
1 four-inch *canela* stick, or 1
   teaspoon ground cinnamon
1 cup sugar

1. A day in advance, turn the rice to powder in a spice grinder or blender set at high speed. Put the rice in a bowl and add the *canela*. Cover with 3 cups boiling water and let stand, overnight, covered with a towel.
2. Pour the mixture into a blender and purée for 3 to 4 minutes. This is a long time, but the mixture cannot be gritty. Add 3 cups water and continue to blend for another minute (in batches, if necessary).
3. Line a large strainer with a double layer of cheesecloth and place it over a large mixing bowl. Pour in the rice mixture, stirring and pressing it through the cloth-lined sieve. When it all passes through, gather the corners of the cloth and squeeze the remaining liquid through, wringing out the cloth.
4. Add the sugar and another 3 cups water. Empty the *horchata* into a large pitcher and refrigerate. Stir before serving ice cold.

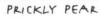

PRICKLY PEAR

Sweetened Cinnamon Coffee
Café de Olla

Coffee bushes can be seen through misty clouds on plantations in Mexico's mountainous states of Veracruz, Oaxaca, and Chiapas. Here's where the country's best coffee is grown before being roasted for a darkly delicious brew. *Café de olla* is what we know as campfire, or cowboy coffee, and it's drunk everywhere in Mexico today—even big-city restaurants offer it in old-fashioned earthenware mugs. Traditionally, *Café de olla* is coarsely ground, then boiled in an earthenware pot along with *piloncillo (panela)* and *canela*. It's drunk black—never with cream. This warming drink is the perfect ending to a home-style *comida* or breakfast at Pilar's minuscule café in Oaxaca City that shares its name with the recipe, Café de Olla (page 214).

Yield: 1 quart

1 quart water

½ to ¾ cup coarsely ground dark roast coffee (not espresso)

4 ounces chopped *piloncillo (panela),* or ½ cup dark brown sugar

2 four-inch *canela* sticks, or 1 cinnamon stick

1. In a nonreactive pot, bring the water to a boil. Add the coffee and, when the water comes back to a boil (the coffee rises), remove from the heat immediately. Add the *piloncillo* and *canela*. Stir to melt the sugar. Let the mixture brew for 3 minutes.

2. Ladle the coffee into mugs through a fine-mesh strainer and serve steaming hot.

Glossary and Table of Equivalents

Achiote. Paste made from annatto seeds (extremely hard, deep red seeds of the annatto tree *Bixa orellana)* and sold throughout markets in Tabasco, Campeche, Chiapas, and Yucatán. In the U.S. you can buy small boxes of this paste at Latino markets—which makes the arduous task of annatto seed grinding a breeze. The seeds are mixed with other seeds and spices such as garlic, cumin, and oregano, then made into *recados* (seasoning pastes) sold in all markets of the Yucatán. The intense orange-red color gets on everything and stains like crazy. Store in the refrigerator.

Acitrón. Candied cactus, eaten as a sweet and also used in cooking.

Adobado. Cooked dish that has been first marinated in *adobo* paste.

Adobo. A marinade, or any food marinated in a chile paste/marinade, either red (guajillo and ancho chiles are most popular) or green (fresh chiles, pumpkin seeds, marjoram, thyme). Most contain garlic, *canela,* vinegar, oregano, cumin, and sometimes tomatoes.

Aguas frescas. Refreshing flavored and sweetened water, served cold and usually iced. The selection list is long—here are some favorites: ruby red from hibiscus flowers; medium brown from tamarind pods; yellow from pineapple; pale green from honeydew melon; bright pink from watermelon; peach from cantaloupe; orange from oranges; pale green from limes; neon chartreuse from green zest of tiny unripened Key limes; neon magenta from special bougainvillea petals; almost white from cucumbers; and gray with tiny chía seeds.

Allspice. The whole, unripe berry of the *Pimenta dioica* tree. Its flavor is similar to that of a combination of cinnamon, cloves, and nutmeg. The whole berry looks like a double-sized black peppercorn. Often sold ground.

Annatto. Seeds of the *Bixa orellana* tree. Brick red, very hard seeds are ground into *achiote* paste for Yucatán's *recado* seasoning paste.

Antojito. Literally "little whim." It's a snack, usually made with *masa,* or tortillas. For example, a taco or tamale eaten from a street vendor's cart is considered an *antojito.* But if numerous tacos or tamales are eaten at home, as a meal, they are no longer called *antojitos.*

Arroz. Mexicans seldom serve plain, steamed rice except in the city of Veracruz and surrounding Gulf towns. Rice is rinsed, dried, and sautéed in oil to coat each grain, then hot broth is poured over: *verde* (green, with herbs); *rojo* (red, with tomatoes); *pilaf* (sautéed with onion); and *amarillo* (yellow, with coloring in Yucatán) are some variations.

Ate. Compressed fruit pastes, usually made with guava or quince. Latino markets carry bricks to be sliced and served, as a dessert, with a smooth cheese such as *panela* or cream cheese with sweet crackers.

Atole. Ancient *masa* gruel made with water or milk, with or without sugar. Mix finely ground *masa harina* into milk, bring to a boil, strain, then add sugar and cinnamon.

Aguacate. Avocado. Fruit from *Persea americana,* a laurel tree family member. Hass (previously spelled Haas) variety is the tastiest, with the best consistency for slicing, dicing, or mashing into guacamole. Hass is usually dark green in markets, then ripens to black (avocados ripen off the tree). The skin is very bumpy. Never refrigerate an avocado unless it is ripe and you can't use it for a few days, or it will be inedible.

Avocado leaves. Claims have been made that U.S. avocado leaves are toxic when eaten in large quantities by small animals. Mexicans have been using them for generations as a flavoring herb—they're similar to anise/bay. When you're in Oaxaca, purchase leaves from wild trees sold by Indian women in open-air markets. (Their anise flavor is stronger than that of U.S. leaves—add fennel tops if using U.S. leaves). Dry them in your hotel room (hang them by their branches over a hanger), then remove the branches and take the leaves back home in plastic bags. Indispensable for some authentic Oaxacan black bean dishes.

Banana leaves. Sold both fresh and frozen in Mexican, Latin American, Caribbean, Filipino, and Asian markets in the U.S. Examine fresh leaves before buying—be sure whole leaves and not irregularly cut pieces are inside the outer leaves. They are huge, about 20 x 40 inches. Frozen leaves are sold in 1-pound packages. Dried leaves (to reconstitute in tepid water) are found in Chinatown. Carefully wipe off any white film with a damp cloth before using. Wash the leaves, then store between layers of moist towels to retain their moisture (and flexibility) while filling. (Purchased leaves are often partially cooked for flexibility. Homegrown leaves need to be parboiled, steamed, or singed before making tamales.) Leaves stay fresh for one week, a few days longer if refrigerated. Old leaves turn yellow, then brown. Banana leaves are used for wrapping and flavoring; they are never eaten.

Bijol. An intensely bright orange coloring agent (corn, flour, cumin, yellow No. 5, red No. 40 and annatto) that gives yellow rice its yellow color. Tiny cans can be purchased in Latino markets and stores that sell Caribbean products, as this is a Caribbean product, adopted by the Yucatán. Substitute turmeric or *achiote* paste diluted with water.

Bolillo. Chewy French roll, about 6 inches x 4 inches with pointed ends, is most often used for *tortas* (sandwiches). The short French reign of Maximilian of Hapsburg (1864-67) brought French bread to the country that claims tortillas as its own. Today most Mexican markets offer both tortillas and *bolillos.*

Botana. Light snack, such as potato chips, olives, pretzels, etc., and most often associated with drinks.

Cajeta. Caramel candy, or sauce, made from goat's milk. Most popular in Celaya, Guanajuato.

Canela. *Cinnamomun zeylanicum,* true Ceylon cinnamon, or Mexican soft cinnamon. Different from, and milder than, the harder stick variety sold in the U.S.

Cazuela. Clay casserole, glazed on the inside, for stovetop or oven baking. Season before use by rubbing with salt and oil, then boiling water in it over direct heat. Rub cloves of garlic on the outside to eliminate any too-earthy tastes; others appreciate this flavor.

Cena. Light supper. After *comida* (full lunch of at least three courses), Mexicans prefer a simple late meal of a tamale or a few tacos, soup, a sandwich, etc., and this often begins as late as 10 P.M.

Chiles. See page 13.

Chirmolera. Green-glazed bowl with a heavy combed texture used for grating the zest of Mexican limes, also known as Key limes.

Chocolate. Mexican chocolate, *Theobroma cacao,* is coarser than European velvety brands such as Lindt, and our Hershey's. Cacao beans are sometimes ground with sugar, *canela,* and often almonds and are used exclusively for hot chocolate to drink and *mole*—never eaten as candy. Have your own recipe ground at a specialty mill in Oaxaca, or buy much less impressive imported brands such as Ibarra and Abuelita. Look for the U.S. brand, LaBelleza, which is excellent. Store in a cool dry place as you would any chocolate.

Chocolate de leche. Hot Mexican chocolate made with milk (or water, *chocolate de agua)* and whipped with a traditional *molinillo.* Drunk from mugs or bowls and often served with sweets, such as egg bread, sweet rolls, or *churros* (doughnuts), in the morning and at night.

Churros. Long, thin doughnuts (12 inches x ½ inch) with ridges, extruded from pastry tubes, fried in oil, and covered with *canela* sugar. They are traditionally dipped into hot Mexican chocolate or black coffee.

Cilantro. *Coriandrum sativum* is also known as Chinese parsley or fresh coriander. The herb is always sold with its roots attached in Mexico.

Cocina callejera. Street food cart.

Comal. Cooking disk made from steel, cast iron, or unglazed earthenware (the last extremely fragile and not a good traveler) for cooking tortillas. Toasting ingredients (see page 28) is an intregal part of southern Mexican cooking and cooks keep a *comal* on the stove, in a permanent position, for this purpose.

Comida corrida. Quickly-served, fixed-menu lunch, including a simple soup, rice or noodles, a main dish, and, sometimes, a bowl of beans. Mexico's blue plate special. *Comida* (late lunch, about 2 P.M.) is most often the main meal of the day in restaurants, coffee shops, market fondas, as well as in homes.

Corn husks. Dried corn leaves used for wrapping tamales.

Crema. Similar to sour cream and French crème fraîche. Huge variations throughout Mexico depend on brands, time of year, location, and age. Color variations from white through ivory, cream, yellow, to rich gold can be seen in markets in dairy-rich areas. Many Mexicans living in the U.S. prefer sour cream, so substituting is no problem except when the recipe calls for the *crema* to be heated or cooked. *Crema* and crème fraîche are both full-fat creams and can be boiled; sour cream curdles.

Desayuno. Light early morning breakfast, usually a sweet roll or bread and a drink. Late breakfast is often called *almuerzo*—it's heavier, with eggs or *chilaquiles*.

Epazote. *Teloxys* (formerly *Chenopodium ambrosioides)* is still a hard-to-find ingredient in the U.S., but it grows like a weed from seeds (no fertilizer and low water) in containers and obscure garden spots. It's now found at many nurseries in 2-inch herb pots during the summer. "The taste and smell," claims a friend, "is like camphor and kerosene." But it grows on you (as cilantro did, remember?), and it's the special ingredient that makes southern Mexican dishes taste regional. There is no substitute.

Escabeche. Pickled or vinegared vegetables found throughout Mexico. Served as a side relish or condiment.

Esquites. Corn kernels boiled with *epazote*. Served in cups from pushcarts in the evening, around *zócalos* from Guadalajara to Toluca, Mexico City, Veracruz, Puebla, and Oaxaca.

Flor de calabaza. Pumpkin blossom.

Fonda. Traditionally, a rooming house or inn, then later a room in a house (or garage) turned into a small neighborhood restaurant. Today, food counters in markets are most often called *fondas,* but are also called *comedors* and *puestos.*

Fry. The verb "to fry," when pertaining to a Mexican sauce, means to heat oil in a deep pot, then carefully pour in liquid (it splatters!), and "fry" the sauce before turning down the heat and simmering (see page 30).

Hierba buena. Spearmint.

Hierbas de olor. Herb bouquet of bay leaf, thyme, and Mexican oregano.

Hoja santa. *Piper auritum,* also known as *acuyo* in Veracruz and southern Gulf areas, and *momo* in Chiapas. Eight-inch, heart-shaped, velvety leaves with an aromatic anise flavor. A good market souvenir: Buy fresh leaves, then spread them out and turn daily so they don't curl, until they're dry. Simply stack or crumble and carry home in a plastic bag.

Horchata. Cold, milky white drink made from rice, *canela,* and sugar. A fine counterbalance for too-spicy chile dishes.

Huitlacoche. Sometimes spelled *cuitlacoche, Ustilago maydis* is a mushroomlike fungus that grows on fresh corn during the summer rainy season. Finest quality is velvety pale gray when raw. Cooked, the color changes to charcoal black. Often prepared with onion, garlic, and chile and stuffed into quesadillas, empanadas, or crepes.

Jamaica. Dried flowers, a variety of hibiscus (sometimes called *roselle)* used to make a bright, garnet red drink prized for its refreshingly sour taste.

Jícama. *Pachyrhizus erosus* is a large tuber, usually about 6 inches across, with a sweet taste and the texture of water chestnuts (when old, jícama is not sweet at all).

Limón. Tiny, juicy, thin-skinned, yellow-green lime known in the U.S. as Key lime. Fruit trees are sold in the Southwest as Mexican lime. Mexicans rarely use yellow lemons.

Maguey. The Spanish name for agave succulent plants grown throughout Mexico. There are more than one hundred species.

Masa. Dough, made from ground (not cut like U.S. cornmeal) dried and hulled corn kernels that have been boiled and soaked in limestone-treated water, and used for tortillas, tamales, and most *antojitos*. Texture can vary from very coarse, for some *gorditas* and tamales, to light and delicate. Typical color varies from dark gold to almost white, with blue corn *masa* popular in central Mexico.

Masa harina. Dried and finely dried ground corn dough *(masa)* is manufactured and sold in the U.S. by The Quaker Oats Company and Maseca. Maseca now produces fine- and coarse-grind *masa harina*. Fine *masa harina* reconstitutes into *masa* for delicate tortillas and banana leaf–wrapped tamales. *Antojitos* such as *gorditas* and *sopes* and most tamales are made with coarse-grind. It's found in Latino markets and many supermarket chains.

Merienda. Afternoon snack, similar to English tea. Most often with Mexican hot chocolate, or coffee, and sweet rolls and fruit.

Metate. Lava rock (basalt) grinding stone of pre-Hispanic origin. Three-legged, sloping-topped, rectangular (about 12 x 24 inches), and with a very heavy grinder *(mano or metlapilli)*, the *metate* is used to grind corn, coffee, and *mole* ingredients. When it's used to grind *cacao* beans or pumpkin seeds, a small fire is lit beneath to heat the ingredients so the oils run easier. Except in the smallest pueblos, these have generally been replaced by electric blenders today, and traditional food texture has suffered.

Mezcal. Alcoholic drink, similar to tequila but generally less refined. Made from the *maguey* (agave) plant *Agave angustifolia*.

Molcajete. Lava rock mortar. Three-legged bowls, often with a spout, for hand-grinding chiles and spices for sauces, with a lava rock *tejolote* (pestle).

Mole. Pronounced mo-LAY, literally translates to "sauce," and there are hundreds in Mexico, originating primarily from the states of Oaxaca and Puebla. Oaxaca claims to be "the home of seven *moles*" and the place from which all other *moles* supposedly sprang. The famous seven are:

> **Mole almendra.** Basically the same as *mole negro* or *rojo,* but with a great amount of blanched almonds, which add flavor and texture, as a *pipián.* Often only ancho chile is used, with cloves, *piloncillo (panela),* and sometimes sesame seeds.

> **Mole amarillo.** Yellow, as the name implies, from chilhuacle chile in Oaxaca (or a combination of guajillo and de árbol chiles), cloves, cumin seed, and, generally, tomatillos. Some cooks in Oaxaca also use chile costeño amarillo. Most often served thin, as a soup, with large chunks of vegetables.

> **Mole chichilo.** Similar to *moles rojo* and *coloradito* but with the addition of anise-flavored avocado leaves, and *masa* as a thickener.

> **Mole coloradito.** A mild red *mole* made with ancho and guajillo chiles only. Nuts, *canela,* and raisins are always included. Many cooks add fried bread to the blender ingredients, as a thickener, along with sesame seeds.

> **Mole negro.** The blackest *mole.* It's made in Oaxaca with chilhuacle negro chile, mulato chile, pasilla chile (the long negro chile—dried chilaca chile—not pasilla de Oaxaca, nor ancho), blackened chile seeds and stems, almonds, sesame seeds, tomatillos, raisins, *canela,* Mexican chocolate, and more.

> **Mole rojo.** Red *mole,* sometimes called *mole colorado,* is brick red. It uses exactly the same ingredients (but there are a million variations) as *mole negro* but the chile seeds and stems are not blackened. Oaxacan cooks use red chilhuacle chile, rather than black. Many cooks add guajillo chile, and some include peanuts.

Mole verde. Green *mole* that gets its color from fresh jalapeño chile, tomatillo, *epazote, hoja santa,* cilantro, flat-leaf parsley, and often thickened with *masa.* It's especially enjoyed in a stew with small *masa* dumplings.

Molinillo. Hand-carved wooden beater for making foamy Mexican hot chocolate.

Nance. (spelled *nanche* in Veracruz, and called *changunga* in Michoacán). Chokecherries, often preserved in sugar syrup, sometimes with alcohol. Found beautifully arranged in large jars in Yucatán, they make fine, if fragile, souvenirs.

Nieve. Literally *"snow,"* this is the name most commonly associated with ice cream and sherbet all over Mexico, and memorably great in Oaxaca and Veracruz. *Nieve* is made with water only for sherbet, or with water and evaporated milk for ice cream *(helado* in many places) with a granita-like, ice-milk texture. Tropical fruit flavors are Mexican national treasures.

Nixtamal. Calcium hydroxide-soaked field corn with skins removed, ready to be ground into *masa.*

Nopales. Cactus paddles (sometimes called cactus leaves) from the *Opuntia* cactus family *(piruli* plant, in Spanish). *Nopalitos* are small, tender *nopales.* Covered with thorns, the paddles must be carefully cleaned before using. Their mucilaginous, slimy texture is similar to that of okra.

Olla. Mexico's ubiquitous clay bean pot. Glazed on the inside only (pots that are glazed on the outside are generally for decorative use). Some have handles and a smaller top section, often with a spout, for making coffee and hot chocolate.

Oregano. True Mexican oregano *(Lippia graveolens)* is sold at weekly markets (there are about a dozen types of wild oregano in Mexico). What is sold in jars in *supermercados* is actually marjoram. McCormick brand in the U.S. is Mexican oregano.

Pan dulce. There's a huge selection of sweet rolls made throughout Mexico, eaten everywhere in the country for breakfast and *merienda* (Mexican afternoon tea).

Panela. See *piloncillo.*

Parsley. Mexicans prefer flat-leaf parsley over curly varieties.

Pepítas. Pumpkin seeds (or squash seeds) used throughout Mexico, especially in the southern states, to grind into *pepián* (pumpkin seed sauce). Raw, roasted, shelled, and unshelled varieties of various sizes are found in all Mexican markets.

Pibil. Vegetables cooked in a Yucatán *pib,* or underground pit. The regional flavoring comes from seasoning paste, called *recado,* and banana leaves.

Piloncillo. Called *panela* in southern Mexico *(panocha* in Sonora), unrefined sugar is pressed into cone or disk shapes and sold in every market. To use, let it dissolve in water, or grate by hand or in a food processor. Substitute dark brown sugar.

Pipián. See pepítas.

Plantains. *Plátanos,* or *machos,* are large, 10- to 12-inch less-sweet versions of our bananas. They are never eaten raw, but are cooked like starchy potatoes when at their green or yellow stages throughout the Caribbean and Mexico's east coast. They are usually sold green and take more than a week to turn completely black, which is when they are at their sweetest. Plantains freeze well, peeled and wrapped.

Postre. Dessert.

Pozole. Soup/stew always containing the large corn kernel, also called *pozole* in Mexico. (U.S. grits are made from this same kernel we call hominy.) The soup's color varies from white to red to green, depending upon the corn's color and regional chiles used.

Pulque. A pre-Hispanic drink made from 100 percent fermented (not distilled) sap of the maguey *Agave salmiana* plant and sold at *pulquerías (pulque* bars), or roadside stands in the countryside. The milky white, mildly alcoholic drink varies in strength by age. *Aguamiel* (honey water) is pure agave juice and a favorite of children—it ferments to *pulque* in two days. *Pulque* is best young and slightly effervescent. Anything older is past it's prime and too strong. Locals often add a splash of bottled hot sauce, a squeeze of lime, and salt.

Queso. Cheese. Some of Mexico's best-known cheeses are listed below starting with fresh and soft, to aged and hard. A dozen types of Mexican cheeses are now being made in the U.S., some brands better than others. Latino grocery stores plus large supermarket chains are the best sources. Also, see Mail-Order Sources (page 204).

> *Requeson.* Fresh cheese. A ricotta texture and flavor. Spreadable. Good to fill enchiladas or to spread on crackers. Similar to hoop cheese.

> *Panela.* Fresh, mild cheese. Clotted curds are drained in baskets to produce its definitive shape. Similar to mozzarella but not as good a melter and slightly saltier. Delicious with fruit or *ate*. Some poorer brands have a squeaky texture.

> *Cuajada.* Fresh cheese. Formed into small football-shaped loaves. Does not melt. Cube or crumble for toppings or fillings.

> *Queso fresco.* Fresh cheese. Also known as *ranchero, queso de metate,* or *adobera.* Generally about 4 inches in diameter and 1 inch thick, it has the texture and taste of very fresh, slightly salty, dry farmer cheese. Does not melt. Cube or crumble over tacos, enchiladas, beans, soups, or salads. It may be sliced to be eaten with fruit. A rinsed, mild feta cheese is a good substitute, as a fresh goat cheese.

> *Asadero.* Cooked cheese. Also called quesadilla cheese everywhere in Mexico. Curds are shaped into a log then sliced. Buttery, smooth taste and firm texture. Substitute Monterey Jack. Flavorful varieties taste like mild domestic provolone. Melts readily.

> *Quesillo de Oaxaca.* Cooked asadero cheese is stretched and rolled into balls, varying from ping pong size to basketballs. Tastes like flavorful string cheese and has the same qualities. Shreds and melts easily. Like *asadero,* it gets stringy when hot.

Chihuahua. Cooked cheese. Also called *queso blanco* or *menonita* (via German Mennonites) cheese. Small, or huge round specimens for cutting off wedges. Substitute mild Cheddar, creamy Munster, or Monterey Jack cheese. Melts fast.

Manchego. Cooked cheese. Golden and round, with a flavor similar to that of Cheddar. Sometimes flavored with herbs. The smooth-textured cheese melts fast.

Enchilado. Firm, dried queso fresco cheese that holds its shape when heated. Aged varieties have hard textures. Strong flavors and fine for grating. Enchilado's distinctive surface has been rubbed with orange-colored chile powder.

Cotija. Also called *queso añejo* (aged) or *queso seco* (dry). An aged, salty queso fresco. Crumbly, salty, and pungent, with a varying texture. *Cotija* can have a soft texture similar to that of feta, or hard as Parmesan depending on the manufacturer and age. Crumble or grate. Romano or Parmesan are good substitutes.

Rajas. Chile strips, usually poblano chile, cooked with onion and eaten in tacos, quesadillas, with scrambled eggs, or as a side dish. Often mixed with *crema.*

Salsa. Sauce, either raw or cooked.

Soplador. Woven palm or rush fan used for stoking fires, and especially coals in braziers under *comales* in rural kitchens or street vendor carts.

Squash blossoms. Bright yellow bouquets of *calabacitas criollas* (pumpkin flowers) are market favorites. They are taken home to be sauced, stuffed, stewed, fried, boiled, and baked—cooked just about any way Mexicans can think of. They can be found in the U.S. at farmer's markets and in gourmet Italian markets. Zucchini blossoms can be substituted, but their orange-green color is different.

Tamal. Tamale to people in the U.S., is just about any food item wrapped in leaves. Most often this means *masa* lightened with vegetable shortening and seasoned, or stuffed with vegetables, often in a chile-flavored sauce, and wrapped with corn or banana leaves. *Tamales* *dulces* are sweetened with sugar, fruit, or dried fruit. Sold and eaten either in the morning, as breakfast, or at night, after 8 P.M., often with the pre-Hispanic drink, *atole.* Leaves are peeled away and discarded before eating the filling.

Tamal steamer. *Tamalerías* are large metal steamers made especially for cooking tamales. A shelf with holes for stacking tamales is placed over boiling water. An opening under the shelf, on the outside of the pot, is for adding water so the lid doesn't have to be removed during the cooking process. *Tamaleros* sell tamales from *tamalerías* in mornings and evenings near *zócalos* and markets. Before making tamales, always be sure you have a system for steaming them. Alternates if you have no *tamalería:* An Asian bamboo steamer, or put an open vegetable steamer over 1 inch of water, unscrewing the center post, if possible; or put 3 water-filled custard cups or empty tuna fish cans at the bottom of a large pot with a nonfragile plate on top (be sure there's enough room for steam to escape along the side). Add 1 inch water, being sure the water does not reach the plate. (Drop a coin into the water before inserting the steamer rack. You know there is water in the steamer as long as the coin rattles.)

Tamarindo. A long brown pod filled with sweet-and-sour-tasting pulp and eaten as a snack. Mixed with water and sugar it makes a refreshing drink enjoyed all over the country.

Tequesquite. Limestone, builder's limestone, or alkaline rocks (calcium hydroxide) used in the preparation of *nixtamal* for *masa.* Also called *cal.*

Tequila. Produced only from *Agave tequilana,* the Weber blue variety. Legally tequila can be produced in only five states: Jalisco, Michoacán, Guanajuato, Tamaulipas, and Nayarit. Jalisco's is considered best. Tequilas made with 100 percent juice, no sugar or water added, are the finest. The town of Tequila is thirty miles west of Guadalajara and an excellent day trip. Recommended reading: *¡Tequila!* by Lucinda Hutson, Ten Speed Press, 1995.

Tianguis. Open-air Indian market, usually held once a week. In towns having a permanent market building but also having a weekly market, the surrounding open-air market on that day is called *tianguis.*

Tienda. Small neighborhood grocery store stocked with daily necessities.

Toast. The verb "to toast" means to char a vegetable, chile, seed, nut, or spice on a hot *comal,* or in a heavy skillet, usually without fat (see page 28).

Tomatillo (or tomate verde). *Physalis ixocarpa* is not part of the tomato family, but is still a fruit. It's a member of the Cape gooseberry family. The tomatillo has a fresh, tart taste and is used in fresh and cooked green salsas and many *moles.* Remove the husks, but never peel before cooking.

Tortilla. See page 22.

Tuna. Prickly pear cactus fruit. Colors vary from green to pink, rose, and ruby-red. Found throughout the country but especially in Jalisco and the central states. An acorn-looking, small, intensely red-meat variety makes Oaxaca's famous *tuna nieve* (cactus fruit sherbet).

Vanilla. *Vanilla planifolia* is a 10-inch, skinny black bean that grows on trees around Papantla, Veracruz, in the northern part of the state. It's the fruit of an orchid and is fermented before drying. Mexico's vanilla is excellent quality, but the country's liquid vanilla is sometimes unhealthful due to chemicals used in processing. In Mexico look for the words "free of coumarin contents" on the label to be sure it's okay.

Verdolagas. Purslane is a ground creeper with fleshy leaves, pinkish stems, and an acidic flavor. Found all over Mexico and often in U.S. farmer's markets.

Vinegar. Mild pineapple vinegar is preferred throughout southern Mexico. Substitute two parts apple cider vinegar and one part water. Yucatecos enjoy the strong flavor of white vinegar.

Zócalo. The town square. Almost every Mexican city and town has one, and it's usually right in front of the main church, and across from city hall.

Table of Equivalents

THE EQUIVALENTS IN THE TABLES HAVE BEEN ROUNDED FOR CONVENIENCE

METRIC

G = GRAM
KG = KILOGRAM
MM = MILLIMETER
CM = CENTIMETER
ML = MILLILITER
L = LITER

US/UK

OZ = OUNCE
LB = POUND
IN = INCH
FT = FOOT
TBL = TABLESPOON
FL OZ = FLUID OUNCE
QT = QUART

OVEN TEMPERATURES

Fahrenheit	Celsius	Gas
250	20	½
275	140	1
300	150	2
325	160	3
350	180	4
375	190	5
400	200	6
425	220	7
450	230	8
475	240	9
500	260	10

WEIGHT MEASURES

US / UK	Metric
1 OZ	30 G
2 OZ	60 G
4 OZ — ¼ LB	125 G
6 OZ	185 G
7 OZ	220 G
8 OZ — ½ LB	250 G
10 OZ	315 G
12 OZ	375 G
14 OZ	440 G
16 OZ —1 LB	500 G
1½ LB	750 G
2 LB	1 KG
3 LB	1.5 KG

LENGTH MEASURES

⅛ IN	3 MM
¼ IN	6 MM
½ IN	12 MM
1 IN	2.5 CM
2 IN	5 CM
3 IN	7.5 CM
4 IN	10 CM
5 IN	13 CM
6 IN	15 CM
7 IN	18 CM
8 IN	20 CM
9 IN	23 CM
10 IN	25 CM
11 IN	28 CM
12 IN - 1 FT	30 CM

LIQUID MEASURES

US	Metric	UK
2 TBL	30 ML	1 FL OZ
¼ CUP	60 ML	2 FL OZ
½ CUP	125 ML	4 FL OZ
1 CUP	250 ML	8 FL OZ
1½ CUPS	375 ML	12 FL OZ
2 CUPS	500 ML	16 FL OZ
4 CUPS - 1 QT	1 L	32 FL OZ

Mail-Order Sources

NEARLY EVERY U.S. CITY HAS A LATINO MARKET THESE DAYS AND their numbers continue to grow by leaps and bounds. With Mexicans moving to the U.S.A. from all corners of their country, we now get food items considered exotica only a few years ago. It's not all that unusual to spot items from Chiapas, Yucatán, or Oaxaca in supermarkets to fulfill the needs of these new immigrants.

If you're looking for a particular imported item, first check the international aisle of your local supermarket, then look in the Yellow Pages under markets, food, bakeries, etc. Within a few minutes of "letting your fingers do the walking" you'll most likely find the name of a Latino place not too far from home.

Fresh produce items such as tomatillos, plantains, avocados, chiles, cactus paddles, coconuts, and mangoes are seasonal standards now, and farmer's markets are supplying unusual items people request, like *epazote*. If you want a certain product, make it known to the growers at these markets and your supermarket manager.

More esoteric products can be mail ordered. The producers and shippers listed here are mail-order pros and ship their items to you in a flash.

Don Alfonso Foods

P.O. Box 201988

Austin, Texas 78720-1988

800-456-6100

Fax 800-765-7373

     Dried ancho, cascabel, guajillo, mulato, pasilla, de árbol, habanero, jalapeño, and chipotle chiles. Don Alfonso makes the very best *chiles chipotles en adobo,* in jars, not cans. Don Alfonso also produces *mole poblano* in 12- and 16-ounce jars, plus *adobo* marinade. Ancho chile paste, chipotle chile paste. Pure chile powders. Annato seed, dried *epazote* and seeds, *cacahuazintle* (Mexican hominy), Mexican oregano, hulled green pumpkin seeds, tamarind, prepared Mexican *achiote* paste. Jars of *chiles en escabeche, nopalitos,* and *cajeta.* Cooking utensils such as *molcajetes,* tortilla presses, *comales,* Mexican lime squeezers, and tamale steamers. Books on Mexican cooking, chiles, and tequila.

Frieda's, Inc.

P.O. Box 58488

Los Angeles, California 90058

800-241-1771

Fax 714-816-0273

     Frieda's is Los Angeles's premier specialty produce supplier, and its products are offered on a daily basis in upscale supermarkets. Frieda's mail-order division sells strictly in full-case orders, and the "availability guide" reads like a *Who's Who* of Mexican food products: dried cascabel, chipotle, habanero, mulato, guajillo, pasilla negro chiles, and an assortment of the last three; fresh chiles such as chilaca, habanero, jalapeño, poblano, serrano, and mixed trays; fresh and dried items including cactus prickly pear fruit and leaves (paddles), papayas, pomegranates, tamarind, a dozen winter squash varieties, chayote (white or green), corn husks, *pozole* (lime-slaked hominy), fresh (or potted) herbs, garbanzo beans, jícama, plantains, and tomatillos.

Melissa's

P.O. Box 21127

Los Angeles, California 90021

800-468-7111 or 800-588-0151

Melissa's is another great source for produce and chiles. Fresh tomatillos, jícama, cactus paddles, and chiles: red and green Anaheim, banana wax, red cayenne, chilaca, orange habanero, Hungarian wax, red and green jalapeño, poblano, and red and green serrano. Dried chiles: ancho, cascabel, chipotle, de árbol, guajillo, habanero, pasilla, pequín, Tabasco, and tepín. Corn husks, pepítas, dried *epazote*, dried Mexican oregano, *canela, jamaica, piloncillo (panela)*, pine nuts, tamarind, tamarind paste, and yucca root.

The CMC Company
P.O. Box 322
Avalon, New Jersey 08202
800-CMC-2780
Fax 609-861-0043

Dried Mexican avocado leaves. Dried Mexican ancho, mulato, pasilla, cascabel, de árbol, chipotle, morita, and habanero chiles. Chile powders. Bottled hot sauces and salsas. Dried Mexican shrimp, Mexican oregano, *piloncillo (panela), achiote* paste, dried *epazote, masa harina*, canned *nopalitos* and tomatillos. Tortilla presses and *comales*.

Adriana's Caravan
409 Vanderbilt Street
Brooklyn, New York 11218
800-316-0820
718-436-8565

Dried herbs and spices from all over the world. Whole allspice, *canela* (true, soft cinnamon), cumin seed, Mexican vanilla beans. Dried whole ancho, guajillo, chipotle, habanero, and pasilla chiles. Chile powders. Canned *chiles chipotles en adobo*. Canned tomatillos. Mexican chocolate tablets. Corn husks.

Herbs of Mexico
3903 Whittier Boulevard
Los Angeles, California 90023
213-261-2521

Dried *epazote*, Mexican oregano, allspice berries, *hoja santa* (called *yerba santa* here), vanilla beans. Over 750 items on the long list.

The Herb Purveyor, Inc.

2315 West Huron

Chicago, Illinois 60612

312-278-1661

> Fresh *epazote* and *hoja* (or *yerba* or *hierba*) *santa* (a.k.a. *acuyo*).

LaBelleza Mexican Chocolate

3200 Corte Malpaso, No. 108

Camarillo, California 93012

805-445-7744 or 888-639-2462

> The very best Mexican chocolate outside Mexico. Made in small batches with tender loving care. Call for special blends, flavors, grinds, and preparation techniques. *Mole negro* exported from Zaachila, Oaxaca.

Gallina Canyon Ranch

144 Camino Escondido

Santa Fe, New Mexico 87501

Fax orders only 505-986-0936

> Elizabeth Berry specializes in beans. About two dozen exotic, antique strains from Mexico and the Southwest. All are open-pollinated by insects and bees. Unusual squash and chile seeds. Sun-dried and smoked chiles.

Santa Barbara Heirloom Nursery

P.O. Box 4235

Santa Barbara, California 93140-4235

805-968-5444

Fax 805-562-1248

e-mail: https//www.heirloom.com/heirloom/

> Organically grown heirloom seeds. An impressive selection of interesting chiles, various culinary herbs, heirloom tomatoes, and "heirloom rainbow tomatoes." Herb wreaths, de árbol chile wreaths, and chile *ristas* interwoven with herbs and raffia so they lay flat against a wall.

Burns Farm

16158 Hillside Circle

Montverde, Florida 34756

407-469-4490

Fax 407-469-3456

Glenn and Roy Burns produce the corn fungus known as *huitlacoche* almost year-round on their central Florida farm. They ship either fresh or frozen *huitlacoche,* depending on the crop at the time of your call, by overnight air express.

Mozzarella Company

2944 Elm Street

Dallas, Texas 75226

800-798-2954

Fax 214-741-4076

Handmade Mexican cheeses: quesillo de Oaxaca and queso fresco. Excellent mozzarella. Try caciotta, the Texas version of Monterey Jack with ancho chile.

Cacique Cheese Co.

Box 729

City of Industry, California 91747

818-961-3399

The Los Angeles cheese firm produces some of the best *crema* in the U.S.A., plus ranchero, panela, cotija, and other Mexican-type cheeses. Products are distributed to New York, Florida, Illinois, Texas, Oklahoma, Kansas, and Arizona—with more states to come—check your supermarket's dairy case.

Manhattan Key Lime Juice Company

118 East 31st Street

New York, New York 10016

212-696-5378

Fax 212-696-9660

Jeanette Richard's company offers bottled pure Key lime juice for the World's Best Margarita (page 179). The juice is all natural and full strength.

Seeds of Change

P.O. Box 15700
Santa Fe, New Mexico 87506-5700
505-438-8080

The seed catalog offers heirloom items not often seen: *tepany* beans from Mexico; *zea mays* Mexican sweet corn; traditional Mexican blue-black corn for blue corn *masa; dent* Oaxacan emerald green corn grown by Zapotecs for green *masa* tamales; green and purple tomatillos; cilantro (coriander seed); and intriguing tomatoes and winter squash.

Hot Stuff

New York, New York
Mail-order only
800-WANT-HOT
Fax 212-254-6120

Dried chiles, canned *chiles chipotles en adobo,* pure chile powders, chile seeds, bottled hot sauces, *epazote,* and annatto seeds.

Coyote Cucina Catalog

1364 Rufina Circle #1
Santa Fe, New Mexico 87501
800-866-HOWL

A catalog filled with fun, well-designed chile gift items (posters, books, clothing, prepared salsas, *molinillos,* etc.). Also dried chiles, *epazote, jamaica,* annatto seed, and pumpkin seeds. *Cajeta,* pure Mexican vanilla, and tamarind paste. The mail-order service is an offshoot of Mark Miller's Coyote Café General Store.

Pendery's

1221 Manufacturing
Dallas, Texas 75207-6506
800-533-1870
Fax 214-761-1966

A mail-order company with retail shops in the Dallas–Fort Worth area. Mexican, Tex-Mex, Southwest—you name it and Pendery's probably has it. Chiles, spices, *jamaica,* cooking equipment, cookbooks, chile and garlic *ristas,* clothing (like a holster for your bottled hot sauces!), and jalapeño-filled bittersweet chocolates.

The Great Southwest Cuisine Catalog

223 N. Guadalupe Street, Suite 197

Santa Fe, New Mexico 87501

800-GREAT-SW (800-473-2879)

Fax 505-466-7124

   Dried chipotle, habanero, ancho, de árbol, guajillo, mulato, and pasilla negro chiles. Or, be first on your block to belong to the Chile of the Month Club. *Cajeta,* pure Mexican vanilla, and Mexican chocolate. Many gift items and baskets.

Mo Hotta-Mo Betta

P.O. Box 4136

San Luis Obispo, California 93403

800-462-3220

Fax 805-545-8389

   The chile-head catalog. Chiles, *achiote* paste, blue corn *atole* flour, corn husks. Prepared salsas, pickled products, fresh habanero chiles, and *masa harina.* Bottled hot sauce heaven: brands such as Vampire Hot Sauce, Dave's Insanity Sauce, Hell Hot, and I Am On Fire Ready To Die. Annatto seeds, Mexican chocolate, *canela* sticks, canned tomatillos. Screamin' Meany Habanero Lollipops for dessert. Cookbooks.

¡Ouchiwawa!

2510-B Main Street

Santa Monica, California 90405

800-WAWAWAS

   Over 200 bottles of hot sauce and more than 75 types of salsa. Northern California's Gil's artichoke or garlic salsa, and Pickled Garlic Company's habanero, red chile, jalapeño, or smoked pickled garlic cloves; and southern California's Adeline's mango salsa—either hot or very hot—perfect for Yucatecan dishes. Great gift baskets. A good selection of Frieda's dried chiles.

Resources: People and Places

I'M PLEASED TO INTRODUCE YOU TO SOME OF MY FAVORITE PEOPLE at top foodie tourist destinations in Mexico. Everyone here enthusiastically helped with this book and generously shared recipes. To make your trips to Mexico all that more enjoyable, everyone speaks English (including people at listed restaurants). Most important, every person goes out of his or her way to make travelers to Mexico feel welcome. They're Mexico's best ambassadors of good will and I hope each of you will meet every one of them someday.

MEXICO CITY
El Bajío
Carmen Ramírez Degollado, owner
Av. Cuitláhuac No. 2709, Colonia Obrero Popular
Tel. 5-341-5877
Every day: 8 A.M. to 7 P.M.

El Bajío restaurant is a quick cab ride from the city center. Go in the morning for tamales and hot Mexican chocolate. Or try lunchtime *antojitos* such as Veracruz-style *gorditas, sopes,* and *tostadas;* or something more substantial such as a matchless *mole de xico* made with black mulato chile, prunes, and plantains from Carmen's hometown near Xalapa, in the state of Veracruz.

Lula Bertrán

Cocina Mexicana

Diego Fernández de Córdoba 135

Mexico, D.F. 11000

Tel. from the U.S. 011-52-5-202-7251

Fax from the U.S. 011-52-5-540-3633

E-mail: abertran@spin.com.mx

Lula is a Mexico City food authority, an editor-consultant of major Mexican food magazines, and a consultant to U.S. companies. She leads foodies on gastronomic tours of the world's largest city. Call or write ahead to book a full day including market and food shop exploring, a cooking class, and all meals.

MICHOACÁN
Su Casa

Marilyn Mayo, owner

Apartado Postal 416

Pátzcuaro 61600

Tel. from the U.S. 011-52-431-10803 (cellular, no answering machine)

Fax from the U.S. 011-52-434-22756

Marilyn, originally from Colorado, lives in her home next to the contemporary rental house, Su Casa, with its breathtaking view of Lake Pátzcuaro. Pátzcuaro is one of Mexico's top centers (behind only Oaxaca) for folk art, and Marilyn's knowledge of the local artisan scene is unequaled. She's a bilingual tour guide *extraordinaira* and takes groups all over Mexico, Guatemala, and Costa Rica.

GUANAJUATO
Bugambilia

Mercedez Arteaga Tovar, owner

Hidalgo No. 42

San Miguel de Allende

Tel. 415/2-01-27

Every day: noon to 11 P.M.

San Miguel de Allende's best traditional restaurant boasts a lovely open courtyard in its colonial building. Specialties from an old San Miguel family's collection of recipes from the rounding regions. Evenings are extra special when a classical guitarist plays.

Reyna Polanco Abrahams Cooking Classes

Reyna Polanco Abrahams, owner

Calle Cri Crí No. 25, Colonia Guadalupe

San Miguel de Allende

Tel. 415/2-41-93

Reyna's cooking classes are held at her spacious home every Friday at noon. Call her to reserve a seat and to find out what she's preparing. Reyna specializes in traditional local dishes as well as specialties from her homeland of Veracruz. If you're interested in meatless dishes, mention it when you call.

El Mesón de San José

Angelika Merkel, owner

Mesones No. 38

San Miguel de Allende

Tel. 415/2-38-48

Every day: 8 A.M. to 9 P.M.

Dine outdoors in a courtyard restaurant surrounded by tasteful boutiques. Breakfasts are first-class, and *huitlacoche* quesadillas under the stars are not to be missed. Try the baked flan with corn kernels for an afternoon coffee break.

OAXACA

Seasons of My Heart

Susana Trilling, owner

Rancho Aurora, Apartado Postal 42, Admon. 3

Oaxaca 68101

Tel. from the U.S. 011-52-951-8-77-26

Susana is originally from the U.S., where she owned a restaurant. She moved to Oaxaca with her Dutch husband to farm beautiful land within sight of Monte Albán. Susana's cooking classes are held at both a Oaxaca City hotel and at her ranch. She also gives tours of Oaxaca's outstanding Indian markets.

El Topil

Soledad Diáz Altamirano, owner

Plazuela La Bastida, No. 104

Tel. 951/4-16-17

Every day: 9 A.M. to 11 P.M.

El Topil restaurant is located on one of the most delightful plazas in Oaxaca, next to Santo Domingo church and around the corner from El Camino Real hotel. Soledad's casual place offers traditional Oaxacan food (some say the *mole* here is one of Oaxaca's best) and is a comfortable place to relax in the evening over a snack and beer.

Café de Olla

Pilar Cabrerea, owner

Reforma 402

Tel. 951/6-11-65

Every day: breakfast, lunch, and early supper to 8 P.M.

This is as close as you'll probably get to sampling Oaxacan home cooking. Café de Olla's *comida corrida,* the afternoon meal, is offered at rock bottom prices at the tiny, spotless café just behind El Camino Real hotel. For large, clean rooms with private baths to rent in a private home, inquire at the café.

BAJA CALIFORNIA
Pancho's

Mary and John Bragg, owners

Hidalgo y Emiliano Zapata S/N

Cabo San Lucas, B.C.S.

Tel. 114/3-09-73

Every day: breakfast, lunch, and dinner

Pancho's world-class collection of tequilas and mezcals could inspire a trip to this fishing heaven at the tip of the Baja peninsula. The restaurant outshines other places in town because of its consistent quality and casual, joyful atmosphere. Try the *chiles rellenos* washed down with a sublime margarita for a quintessential Cabo experience.

Index

641.5636 Zaslavsky, Nancy.
Z
    Meatless Mexican home
    cooking.

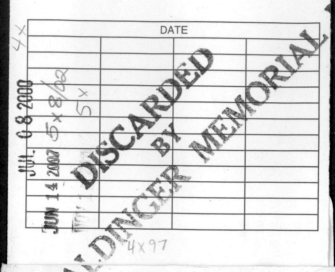

DATE			

JUL 08 2000

JUN 14 2007

5 x 8/00

5 x

4 x

4 x 97

APR 25 1997

DO NOT TOUCH THE DATE CARD

BAKER & TAYLOR